WORSHIP
CONNECT
SERVE

An Introduction to Covenant Membership in
Cornerstone Apostolic Church

STEVE PIXLER

WORSHIP
CONNECT
SERVE

An Introduction to Covenant Membership in
Cornerstone Apostolic Church

STEVE PIXLER

Published by
Continuum Ministry Resources
5200 David Strickland Rd Fort Worth TX 76119

Published in the United States by
Continuum Ministry Resources
5200 David Strickland Rd.
Fort Worth, TX 76119

Printed in the United States of America

Cover design by Derrick Pulley

ISBN13: 978-0-9796261-2-8
ISBN10: 0-9796261-2-9

Library of Congress Control Number: 2011934611

TABLE OF CONTENTS

Introduction   7

Part One: *Worship*   13
    1. Worship In Oneness   15
    2. Worship On the Lord's Day   27
    3. Worship as a Way of Life   41
    4. Worship as War   49

Part Two: *Connect*   59
    5. Connecting as the Body of Christ   61
    6. Connecting through Koinonia   77
    7. Edifying the Body   97
    8. The Communion of the Saints   107

Part Three: *Serve*   121
    9. Christian Service and the Kingdom of God   123
    10. Serving the Family   135
    11. Serving the Church   147
    12. Serving the World   161

Appendix A   175

Introduction

Welcome

Welcome to **Worship** → **Connect** → **Serve**, the "Members-to-Missions Class" of Cornerstone Apostolic Church. Those who enroll in the **Worship** → **Connect** → **Serve** Teaching Series have either recently experienced baptism or are transferring membership to our local congregation. Either way, **Worship** → **Connect** → **Serve** is the series that introduces to you the vision and mission of Cornerstone Church and transforms you from merely a "member" to an active, engaged "missionary" in your world. Our primary objective here is to properly orient new members toward the mission of Cornerstone Church.

Cornerstone Church is not just another place to attend Sunday services. God has called us to fulfill a mission to and for the city of Fort Worth and surrounding communities. Many people choose to attend church based on personal preference, because they like the music, the fellowship, the preaching, or, maybe even because it is close to home. And, no doubt, much of that is important. But membership at Cornerstone demands more. Membership demands mission.

Covenant Members

Membership at Cornerstone compels a deep commitment to the mission of the church, both the eternal vision of the universal church that the apostle Paul explained in *The Epistle to the Ephesians* and the particular vision of this local church that is explained in this course. This course details the vision that motivates this mission, and before we are finished, you will be called to enter into a covenant with Cornerstone Church to live out that vision through your personal mission. All members at Cornerstone are covenant members. That is, every member here is called to enter into a covenant with fellow believers to share in a unified passion for worship, fellowship and Christian service in and to the world.

The covenant mission of Cornerstone Church is three-fold. First, we covenant together to **WORSHIP** the one true God in such a way that all nations will come to worship Him as God revealed in Christ through the Holy Spirit. Second, we covenant together to **CONNECT** with one another in such a way that we truly edify the body of Christ and meet the needs of those Christ has saved. Third, we covenant together to **SERVE** our families, our church and the world in such a way that the love of God in Christ through the Holy Spirit is truly actualized in the real world.

THE GROWTH CONTINUUM

Our covenant moves us forward in a three-stage cycle. First, we learn to **WORSHIP**, and we grow in the grace of glorifying the Father in Christ through the Spirit. Then, we learn to **CONNECT** and build deep, lasting relationships with fellow Christians, benefiting from the gifts of others while contributing our own gifts for the good of the entire body. Finally, we are equipped, empowered and emboldened to **SERVE** in the world as the mediated presence of God in Christ through the Spirit to the world around us.

Of course, we do not mean that Christians cannot connect and serve until they have finished their training in worship, or that they cannot serve until they connect. By no means. Every born again Christian is immediately called to worship God, connect with the church and serve the world on a basic, introductory level. Yet, it is true that we discover a powerful momentum that propels a steady process by which we grow deeper into further stages of Christian ministry and mission. And this development will move us forward along this growth continuum:

WORSHIP → CONNECT → SERVE

As we grow in Christ, we will find ourselves returning to this cycle of growth again and again. As we serve the Lord over a long period of time, there will be periods of spiritual stagnation when we seem to stall in our Christian growth. *In every case*, you will be pulled back on track by the Holy Spirit as He compels you back to the basics of putting **WORSHIP** first; then, seeking to re-**CONNECT** with the people of God; and, finally, recovering your focus on your mission to **SERVE** the world around you. We cannot forget this cycle of growth:

WORSHIP → CONNECT → SERVE

COVENANT OF GRACE

Before we proceed further in our study, we should pause to assert that this covenant is a covenant of grace, which means that we do not think for a moment that we can empower ourselves to excel in these three stages of Christian growth. No, we humbly and gratefully acknowledge that salvation and sanctification is *sola gratia,* by grace alone, which means that we trust in the power of God's free gift of salvation to propel us along this continuum. Thus, we do not expect our members to enter into a covenant with Cornerstone Church to **WORSHIP, CONNECT** and **SERVE** in their own strength.

This pressure to keep this covenant in human strength would crush the strongest Christian. Faithfulness requires the faithfulness of Christ at work in us through the indwelling power of the Spirit. We exhort every member of the body to be filled daily with the Spirit, and to "work out your own salvation with fear and trembling, for it is God who works in you, both to will and to work for his good pleasure" (Philippians 2:12, 13).

THE TEMPLE OF GOD

The church of Jesus Christ is the temple of the living God. In one sense, we can say that all creation is the temple of God, for "Thus says the LORD: 'Heaven is my throne, and the earth is my footstool; what is the house that you would build for me, and what is the place of my rest?'" (Isaiah 66:1) Yet, when the church is gathered to worship, it becomes the spiritual intersection of heaven and earth. As the psalmist said, God is "enthroned on the praises of Israel" (Psalm 22:3). Heaven is the throne of God, but earth receives His resident glory when the church gathers to worship.

Since God first gave instructions on how to build an altar in His name, the people of God have gathered at His temple to **WORSHIP → CONNECT → SERVE.** The people of God were called together to **WORSHIP** the one true God; to

10

assemble and **CONNECT** as the congregation of God; and to go out from the presence of the Lord to **SERVE** the world by displaying the glory of God to the nations. There is no better example of this three-fold purpose than the story of Isaiah's vision of God recorded in Isaiah 6:1-8:

> **WORSHIP** (1) In the year that King Uzziah died I saw the Lord sitting upon a throne, high and lifted up; and the train of his robe filled the temple. (2) Above him stood the seraphim. Each had six wings: with two he covered his face, and with two he covered his feet, and with two he flew. (3) And one called to another and said: "Holy, holy, holy is the LORD of hosts; the whole earth is full of his glory!"

> **CONNECT** (4) And the foundations of the thresholds shook at the voice of him who called, and the house was filled with smoke. (5) And I said: "Woe is me! For I am lost; for I am a man of unclean lips, and I dwell in the midst of a people of unclean lips; for my eyes have seen the King, the LORD of hosts!" (6) Then one of the seraphim flew to me, having in his hand a burning coal that he had taken with tongs from the altar. (7) And he touched my mouth and said: "Behold, this has touched your lips; your guilt is taken away, and your sin atoned for."

> **SERVE** (8) And I heard the voice of the Lord saying, "Whom shall I send, and who will go for us?" Then I said, "Here am I! Send me."

Isaiah worshipped the one true God. Then, he recognized in the holy presence of God that he was guilty and that all his people shared his guilt. Isaiah was inescapably connected to his people. Finally, the voice of God thundered out a "third-stage" mission: "Whom shall I send, and who will go for us?" Isaiah replied—as we must all reply still today—"Here am I! Send me."

It is not enough to simply worship God. We must connect with the people of God. And it is not enough just to worship God and connect with the church; we must go out in the power of the revelation received in worship and the strength received in fellowship and serve the world around us. This is what this course is all about:

WORSHIP → CONNECT → SERVE

CONCLUSION

Has God called you to participate in this mission? Do you feel God has called you to worship Him, to connect with the church, and to serve the world around you? It is the unique way that Cornerstone worships, connects and serves that sets our congregation apart. We invite you to share in that unique way of being the church. There are no limits to the possibilities of what God can do through us if we can catch His vision for us as individuals, for our families and for our church—indeed, for the world. We will spend the next twelve weeks together casting the vision of **WORSHIP → CONNECT → SERVE.** Do you feel called to participate in this mission? We pray that somewhere along the way the Holy Spirit will transform us all from merely members to missionaries!

PART ONE: WORSHIP

Chapter One

Worship in Oneness

One God, One People, One Worship

The fundamental fact of Christian worship is that we worship one God. This is the first thing that any discussion of Christian worship must emphasize. Israel was commanded to teach their children daily, "Hear, O Israel: the Lord our God is one Lord" (Deuteronomy 6:4 KJV). And because we worship only one God, we are formed as the people of God into one, unified worshipping community. The oneness of God produces the oneness of His people through the oneness of worship. The apostle Paul makes this point in Romans as he argues for the unity of Jews and Gentiles within one Christian church:

> Or is God the God of Jews only? Is he not the God of Gentiles also? Yes, of Gentiles also, since God is one. He will justify the circumcised by faith and the uncircumcised through faith. (Romans 3:29, 30)

Paul's point is very simple: if there is only one God, then all nations must come to worship Him alone. There is no other God to worship. *Period.* Paul sees the oneness of God as the basis for global evangelism, the preaching of the gospel in every nation under the heaven. Because there is only one God, and thus, only one people of God, then all the nations must forsake their false gods, which are nothing more than lying images, and come together into one church to worship the one true God. Then, this unified worship draws all people, regardless of their various religious, economic and political backgrounds, into a unified Christian community. This is how the oneness of God produces the oneness of worship that produces the oneness of the church.

Paul envisions a church made up of people from every nation under heaven worshipping the one true God throughout the entire world no matter their ethnic background, no matter their diversity of culture or creed. Moreover, the diversity of the nations is not lost in a Christian homogenization of global culture. Rather, when the Holy Spirit is poured out on all flesh, baptizing and converting members of every culture under heaven, each individual is brought into the service of the kingdom of God contributing his or her God-given gifts in their own unique cultural expression. These multicultural gifts are like individual threads woven into the rich fabric of Christian life. The oneness of worship produces unity, but it is unity-in-diversity.

ONE GOD AS FATHER, SON AND HOLY SPIRIT

The one God that we worship has revealed Himself as Father, Son and Holy Spirit. It is important to understand this initially as we consider the worship of the one true God, because worship that does not see God as Father, Son and Holy Spirit is not true worship. The fullness of this divine self-revelation is embodied in the person of Jesus Christ, in whom dwells "the fullness of the godhead bodily" (Colossians 2:9).

Misconceptions of God abound. There are those that profess to worship the one true God, but they deny the deity of the Son of God, Jesus Christ, and wrongly claim that He was just a man, maybe a prophet or a sage, but just a man. There are others that profess to worship the one true God that deny Jesus altogether and blaspheme Him as a pretender and fraud. Sadly, this means that their worship of God is not true worship at all, for Jesus said that no can come to God except through Him (John 14:6). We cannot worship God as Christians if we refuse to worship Jesus as Christ.

The one true God is the Father, and He is a Spirit that has no essential, fleshly form. However, the Father revealed Himself as "image," which, Paul teaches, is the Son of God, Jesus Christ (Colossians 1:15; see also Hebrews 1:3). Prior to the birth of Jesus Christ, the event commonly called the "incarnation" of God in Christ, the Son of God was known as the "Word" of God, the "Logos" of God (John 1). This is how the writer of Hebrews can say that the "Son of God" created all things, even though the fleshly, physical form of Christ did not come into visible existence until Jesus was born at Bethlehem. Jesus exists eternally with the Father as the Word of the Father. Thus, Jesus says, "Whoever sees me has seen the Father" (John 14:9). Jesus is the only image of God that we shall ever see.

God not only reveals Himself as "the Son of God," but He reveals Himself as "the Holy Spirit," which is simply the Spirit of God the Father flowing out of Himself through Christ into the church and through the church into all creation. Thus, to deny the Holy Spirit is to deny God Himself. We must embrace God as Father, Son and Holy Spirit in order to know Him as the one, true God. To deny the Son or the Spirit is to deny the Father. "These three are one" (I John 5:7 KJV).

One of the reasons it is so important to worship God as Father, Son and Holy Spirit is because that is exactly *how* we worship Him. We worship God in Christ through the power of the Holy Spirit. As Paul said, "For we are the circumcision, which worship God in the spirit, and rejoice in Christ Jesus, and have no confidence in the flesh" (Philippians 3:3). Here (and elsewhere), we see that we worship God through the Spirit in the person of Christ. If we deny the Holy Spirit, then our worship never ascends beyond our human spirit, for the Holy Spirit takes hold of the worship (or prayer, praise and any other form of devotion) within our spirit and lifts it up in the person of Christ, who, as our ever-living intercessor, presents our worship in the presence of God. As Hebrews says, "Consequently, he is able to save to the uttermost those who draw near to God through him, since he always lives to make intercession for them" (Hebrews 7:25).

Paul makes this point in a powerful way in Romans 8:34 concerning prayer, but the point is valid for worship as well. In fact, prayer is really just another aspect of worship, broadly considered. When the revelation of God as Father, Son and Holy Spirit is distorted, then our worship is inevitably distorted.

WORSHIP AND PRAISE

To worship God is to bow before Him and offer Him thanks for His blessings and give Him glory for His greatness. We are all called to worship God and give Him the highest praise. Now, there is a slight distinction in Scripture between worship and praise. No doubt there are many ways that worship and praise blend into one devotional experience, but when we study the words "worship" and "praise" more closely there is somewhat of a difference between them. To put it simply, worship nearly always means to fall down before God with reverence and humility, while praise nearly always means to rise up, even *leap* up, and lift up exuberant shouts of joy.

Worship is more often "reverence," while praise is more often "rejoicing." This is important to note now because too often Christians tend to reduce worship down to either reverence *or* rejoicing, and a large part of the Christian celebration is lost. God calls us to be reverent at times and to rejoice at other times.

The heart and soul of worship is thanksgiving and glory. When we worship God, we offer thanks for His blessings and give Him glory for His greatness. To offer thanks is to focus on the good things God has done for us. But to lift up glory to God is to focus on how great God is apart from any consideration of all He has done for us. And both aspects, thanksgiving and glory, are essential to balanced worship.

Praise carries worship a step further and rises up to celebrate the goodness and greatness of God with loud shouts of joy, with music, singing and dancing. When we gather to worship and praise the Lord, our experience should run the gamut of emotions, from calm, quiet reverence to loud, boisterous—even raucous!—rejoicing.

And "the gamut of emotions" is exactly the right way to say this, because the whole man, including the emotions of man, must be engaged in worship. God desires worship that is more than just a quiet, intellectual consideration of the nature of God. The Lord wants His people to worship Him with their whole heart—with their heart, soul, mind and strength. Anything less is less than worship.

WORSHIP IN THE TEMPLE OF GOD

When we worship, we stand in the temple of God giving glory to God as God's image. This is one of the reasons why God forbade man to make images of Him, for Christ Jesus alone is the perfect image of God. In fact, Adam was made in the likeness of Christ who was to come. Therefore, any image of God made by man falls far below any sort of accurate depiction of who God really is. An idol freezes man's limited perception of God into wood or stone and perpetuates a lie about God.

The Psalmist said that man was "fearfully and wonderfully made" to highlight the glory that God shares with man. In contrast, the prophet mocked the idols made by man for their shallow glory that fades with the rotting wood or corroding metal from which they are made. The only image that God will permit in His temple is man, the image of God.

The temple of God is any place where God is truly worshipped. On one hand, the temple of God spreads across the vast expanse of the cosmos, across the entire universe. On the other hand, the temple of God is established within believers, for our bodies are the temple of God. Each believer is an individual temple of God, but no believer is the temple of God alone. Each believer is an individual temple only as they are connected by the Spirit into the body of Christ.

So, in one sense, our *body* (singular) is the temple of the Holy Spirit, but in another sense, our *bodies* (plural) are the temple of the Holy Spirit. Both aspects are true, and both aspects are vitally important. (See Romans 12:1 where Paul teaches that our many "bodies" are one "living sacrifice.")

As the image of God, the church serves God in His holy temple in three offices: first, the church serves as *priests* of God through the ministry of intercession; second, the church serves as *prophets* of God through the ministry of preaching and teaching the Word of God, and through the ministry of the gifts of the Holy Spirit at work in the church; and third, the church serves as *kings* through "binding and loosing," "remitting" and "retaining" sins through baptism and communion. (More on that later.)

When we see worship as "worship in the temple of God," and we see ourselves as standing in the temple as the only image of God that the world will ever see, then we understand better why we must present worship as an offering that pleases God and attracts the world to Him.

WORSHIP IN SPIRIT AND TRUTH

One of the most important passages on worship is John 4. Every Christian should read this passage and often and commit as much as possible to memory, especially the part about worshipping "in spirit and in truth." This passage contains one of the most radical statements about worship in the entire Bible. Jesus told the woman of Samaria that worship would no longer be restricted to Mt. Zion in Jerusalem (where the Jews worshipped) or to Mt. Gerizim near Samaria (where the Samaritans worshipped).

Jesus did not say that the Jews were wrong to worship at Jerusalem. In fact, Jesus emphasized the fact that "salvation is of the Jews," which was a major dispute between Jews and Samaritans. However, the important part—indeed, the radical part—is that Jesus announced that "the time has come" when worship would be decentralized away from any particular geographical location to wherever believers gather to worship the Father "in spirit and in truth."

This transition in worship began at this time because of the advent of Christ as Messiah and the coming outpouring of the Spirit of God upon all flesh at Pentecost. In fact, the "time" that had come was a long-awaited time to which worship at the temple had pointed all along. Worship that is centered in the human heart and flows out through a Spirit-filled community of believers into all creation was God's ultimate goal for worship all along. The temple-centered worship of the Old Covenant was simply a "type and shadow" of the worship to come.

Therefore, we must worship the Father in Spirit and in truth. This can be taken at least a couple of ways: first, we must worship in the power of the Holy Spirit (Spirit) according to the direction of the Word (truth); second, we must offer worship that flows out of our human spirit (spirit) with sincerity and honesty (truth) before God. Of course, there is no reason to choose one approach over the other: they are both correct. We must offer worship to God that flows out of our human spirit empowered by the Holy Spirit, and this worship must conform to both the Word of truth, the Scriptures, and be sincere and honest before God.

This sort of worship draws like-minded people together into one worshipping community of believers. No longer is the faith community gathered around a building or a temple, but we are gathered around the presence of Christ mediated through the Holy Spirit. When believers are gathered together to worship in Spirit and truth, it produces the unity of the Spirit that Jesus prayed for in John 17 and Paul spoke about in Ephesians 4.

THE UNITY OF THE SPIRIT

Remember now: we are considering worship from the standpoint of God's oneness and the oneness of His people that flows out of His oneness. If God is one, then His people must be one. And it is the one worship of that one God that forms one body. We are one because we worship as one.

This is why Jesus prayed so fervently for the unity of His church in His high-priestly prayer in John 17. God is making all things new as He makes all things one. Paul tells us in Ephesians 1:10 that the oneness of all things, of everything in heaven and in earth, is the eternal purpose of God.

God does nothing in the earth that is not driven by this unity impulse. When the church was established and filled with the Spirit, the driving motive of the Spirit was to gather His people into one holy nation throughout the earth. God is on a divine vendetta against division, against the division of the human heart, the human family and the human race that came as a result of sin and death.

Of course, all division is rooted in man's division from God, and thus, reconciliation—which is the re-alignment of all things in perfect unity—must first occur between God and man. When God and man have been reconciled, and this happened at the cross, then men may be reconciled to one another. This perfect unity is the one God's keenest desire.

However, the point to be emphasized now is that this unity flows out of unified worship. When we worship in Spirit and in truth, we join together in the unity of the Spirit.

Look at Paul's list of the seven "ones" of Ephesians 4:3-6:

> Endeavoring to keep the unity of the Spirit in the bond of peace. There is one **body**, and one **Spirit**, even as ye are called in one **hope** of your calling; One **Lord**, one **faith**, one **baptism**, One **God** and Father of all, who is above all (transcendent), and through all (mediated) and in you all (immanent). (Emphasis and comments added.)

Paul declares that this "unity of the Spirit" leads to "the unity of the faith" (Ephesians 4:13). Paul knew very well that the church of his day was grievously divided over many issues, and he knew that this was not God's goal for His people. Yet, Paul did not despair over the state of the church, because he knew that the Holy Spirit, which is Christ Jesus mediated to believers and through believers to the world, was inexorably drawing together the people of God into one, full-grown, mature body of believers.

Paul trusted in the sovereign power of God to build the church through the ascension of Christ and the outpouring of His Spirit at Pentecost. And Paul knew that this unity was flowing out of the body gathered for worship. This is the central point of Ephesians, that the church is being built as

God's holy habitation, His temple, through the Spirit. One God, one Spirit, one church, one faith. All is one.

CONCLUSION

We cannot underestimate the power of unified worship. We are called to worship one God as one people so that all creation may be made one in Christ. We shall consider more of this idea when we look at "connecting" as the body of Christ. But for now, we must emphasize that our mutual "connecting" is based on our mutual worship of the one true God. We are not joined together because we share a common language, culture, tradition or race. We are joined together because we worship the same God. Let us worship Him in Spirit and in truth.

CHAPTER TWO

WORSHIP ON THE LORD'S DAY

WHY DO WE WORSHIP ON THE LORD'S DAY?

Weekly, Sunday worship is the traditional practice of historic Christianity. But is there a biblical pattern for it? The Bible does not explicitly teach weekly worship on Sunday, but we can trace clear biblical outlines for our practice. We shall see the same for the patterns of The Lord's Service and The Lord's Supper.

Many groups such as Adventists and others have rejected the idea of Sunday worship as a Roman Catholic corruption of true worship. This claim must be examined in light of Scripture and church history. We shall confine our examination to the precedent of Scripture, but the point of respectfully considering historical church practice is a valid one (I Corinthians 7:17, 11:16; 14:33, 34; 16:1; I Thessalonians 2:14).

The Practice of the Early Church

At first, the early church worshipped day by day, attending the temple together and breaking bread in their homes (Acts 2:42, 46). Then, a developing pattern of weekly worship is discernible in the biblical record.

On the first day of the week, when we were gathered together to break bread, Paul talked with them, intending to depart on the next day, and he prolonged his speech until midnight. (Acts 20:7)

Now concerning the collection for the saints: as I directed the churches of Galatia, so you also are to do. On the first day of every week, each of you is to put something aside and store it up, as he may prosper, so that there will be no collecting when I come. (I Corinthians 16:1, 2)

I was in the Spirit on the Lord's day, and I heard behind me a loud voice like a trumpet (Revelation 1:10)

Why did the early church establish the pattern of hallowing the first day of the week unto the Lord? How did Sunday become "the Lord's Day"?

First of all, they worshipped on Sunday because the resurrection of Jesus was on the first day of the week, on Sunday, and the worship of the church is the celebration and witness of the resurrection of Jesus Christ.

Second, Jesus appeared several times to the disciples after His resurrection, and it seems to have been His preference to visit with them on the first day of the week (John 20: 1, 19, 26). John clearly structures chapter 20 to highlight the "first day pattern" of assembly together with Jesus.

Third, it seems that Jesus ascended on the first day of the week as He gathered with His disciples on the mountain.

Fourth, though there is some disagreement about this, the Feast of Pentecost was celebrated by Israel on the first day of the week (Leviticus 23:11), and thus, the Day of Pentecost, when the Holy Spirit was poured out, was on Sunday. This would have further established the theological and spiritual significance of the first day in the minds of early believers.

The Sabbath Pattern

Moreover, the early church seemed to have understood something about the Sabbath pattern for worship and its fulfillment in the New Covenant. God created the earth in six days, and on the seventh day He rested from His labors. He hallowed the seventh day and commanded His people to acknowledge His sovereign rest by joining with Him in rest each Saturday.

Then, when God called Israel out of Egypt and formed them into a holy nation of kings and priests, He commanded them to gather each seventh day in a "holy convocation," which became the basis for weekly synagogue worship (Leviticus 23:3). The early church was made up of only Jews at first, and they would have readily embraced the idea of weekly worship. Indeed, at first, they worshipped on *both* the seventh day (in the Jewish synagogues) *and* the first day (in the Christian assemblies).

However, it is obvious that the early church grew in their understanding of how the Sabbath was to be understood in the New Covenant. According to Paul in Colossians 2, and Hebrews 3 and 4, the Old Covenant Sabbath still has spiritual significance for the New Covenant church, but only in the sense that *it is fulfilled in Christ.*

According to Paul in Colossians 2, the Sabbath was nailed to the cross of Christ, and is thus dead, buried and resurrected in Him. This is how, as the early church came to understand the full implications of Christ's resurrection and the New Covenant signed, sealed and delivered in Christ, they came to see the Sabbath as "born again" in the New Covenant as the Lord's Day.

This is why Paul was so adamant that we should never allow anyone to "disqualify" us on the basis of Sabbath-keeping or observing Jewish feast days (Colossians 2:16). To go back and observe the Old Covenant Sabbath is to deny its fulfillment in Christ. To do so is to dance with shadows. Thus, the early church realized that seventh-day worship had passed away in Christ. Worship on the first day of the week fulfills the Old Covenant pattern while recognizing the reality of the new creation.

HOW DO WE WORSHIP ON THE LORD'S DAY?

Probably the most important thing we can learn about worship is that our worship on earth is intended by God to reflect the worship in heaven. Jesus emphasizes this reality in the prayer that He taught us to pray daily, the Lord's Prayer: "Your kingdom come. Your will be done *in earth as it is in heaven.*" The kingdom of God breaks in upon the earth when believers worship God in a way that manifests heaven to earth. When we worship, the eyes of every man, woman and child should be turned to behold the glory of God shining from the heavens. Does our worship look like heaven?

Mediatorial Worship

The Lord's Day is the celebration of the new creation that is coming but has already come in the church. This means that our worship should be patterned after the future reality of God's universal rule in Christ. The Lord's Day is an anticipation of *The Day of the Lord* when God assembles His people and judges the world (Matthew 18; I Corinthians 5, 6). When we gather, we gather to minister as *priests* (to make intercession for the world); as *kings* (to minister judgment, which is discernment, for the world); and as *prophets* (to minister revelation, which is direction, for the world).

When we worship we stand between the present and the future to mediate the coming kingdom, the new creation that has already broken in upon the world in the resurrection of Christ in this present evil age. When we worship, we stand between the kingdom of God and the kingdom of darkness to push back its control in the earth, the control that has already been demolished in Christ at the cross. When we worship, we stand between God and man to represent God to man and man to God. Worship is mediation.

Liturgy

Because Christian worship is arranged according to the order of worship in heaven, we must carefully consider the way we approach God each Sunday. Moses was commanded to build the tabernacle, which expressed the proper order for approaching God in its design and layout, "according to the pattern that was shown [him] on the mountain" (Hebrews 8:5).

Paul taught the church at Corinth that worship was to be done "decently and in order" (I Corinthians 14:40). The word "order" here is the Greek word *taxis*, which means "rank" or "course." In the Temple, the priests served after their "course"—their *taxis*. Paul is saying here that our worship must mature beyond the disorder that characterizes pagan worship and grow into the order of worship that honors God and brings glory to His name. Our worship should never embarrass heaven.

The order of worship is called "liturgy." This word is derived from the Greek word *leitourgos,* which means "priest" or "officiant" in Temple worship. The word "liturgy" is sometimes misunderstood by those in the Free Church tradition as describing formal, ritualistic worship that is dead and devoid of the Spirit. However, the word is biblical, and the idea of order in worship is biblical.

In fact, every church, whether "free church" or "high church," has a liturgy. It may be formal or informal, written out or simply followed by common impulse and settled tradition, but all crowds tend to gravitate toward settled patterns of behavior in order to avoid pure chaos. This is human nature, and it is a part of human nature that reflects the orderly impulse of the image of God within us.

So, the question is not *if* we shall follow a liturgy, but rather *what* liturgy shall we follow? It is our conviction at Cornerstone Church that we must look to the patterns of worship revealed in Scripture and seek to continually conform our earthly worship to the worship offered to God in heaven.

The Pattern of Worship in the Early Church

In order to get a snapshot of New Covenant worship, let's look briefly at Acts 2:42, where the pattern of early worship is laid out.

> And they devoted themselves to the apostles' teaching and fellowship, to the breaking of bread and the prayers. (Acts 2:42)

There are four things listed here, each with the definite article "the" before it to signify that these were particular, formal elements of worship:

The Teaching. The early church established their fledgling faith community on a solid foundation of examining the Scriptures and teaching the gospel of Jesus Christ as the fulfillment of all that is found there. As Paul taught the church at Corinth, there is no substitute for the preaching of the Word (I Corinthians 1-4). We are saved by preaching (Romans 1:16; I Corinthians 15:2, etc.). God has "manifested in his word through the preaching" (Titus 1:3). When we gather to worship, we must give preaching priority, just as being placed at the head of the list emphasizes it here.

The teaching of the Word, however, includes much more than just the Sunday sermon. It includes the public reading and explanation of Scripture. Paul told Timothy to "devote yourself to the public reading of Scripture, to exhortation, to teaching" (I Timothy 4:13).

Teaching is done through prophecy as the prophets, whom we would call "preachers" today, stand in the congregation to encourage and exhort the people of God (I Corinthians 14).

Teaching is done through singing: "Let the word of Christ dwell in you richly in all wisdom; teaching and admonishing one another in psalms and hymns and spiritual songs, singing with grace in your hearts to the Lord" (Colossians 3:16).

There are manifold ways that the Word of God is taught in the worship service. However it is done, it *must* be done.

The Fellowship. The early church continued steadfastly in *the fellowship.* Now, when we think of fellowship, we tend to think only of social interaction when we gather to eat and visit together. However, fellowship in the New Testament entails much more than that. The word translated "fellowship" comes from the Greek word *koinonia.* Learn this word, for we use it often here to describe the life of the church community and the care that we show for one another each Sunday and every day.

Koinonia is a word packed with meaning, and this makes it somewhat difficult to define. Probably the best way to sum it up is to say that koinonia is "mutual care." The Hellenistic (Greek) world of the first century used koinonia to describe the many societies and clubs that were formed for the mutual care and welfare of their members. These clubs were often guilds or unions that joined laborers, artists, artisans and craftsmen together. So, when you spoke of koinonia in the first century, you spoke of *belonging.*

When you joined a society and shared koinonia, it meant that someone was there to lift you up when you were down, to befriend you and fight for your cause. It also meant that you could expect financial help when times were tough. If you died unexpectedly, the society would join together and take care of your burial and help your surviving widow and children. And much, much more.

However, the point here is that koinonia means more than just getting together for a social event. It means to join a society of people that will see that you belong, that you receive mutual care. This is what the early church did, and it is what we must do.

Koinonia is more than horizontal fellowship between believers; koinonia also has a vertical aspect when we fellowship with one another in Christ. The "fellowship" includes fellowship with God in a loving, mutual relationship. We will talk more about the details of this when we take a closer look at **CONNECT** below.

The Communion. The "breaking of bread" here is *the* breaking of bread. The definite article "the" in the original text indicates that this is more than just an ordinary meal. We can contrast verse 42 with 46, where they "broke bread from house to house" to see the distinction (there is no definite article "the" in verse 46 in the original text). "The breaking of bread" in verse 42 is communion.

It seems likely that the early church celebrated communion every time they gathered for worship. The pattern of weekly communion developed as the pattern of weekly worship developed. There is evidence here in Acts 2:42 and elsewhere that communion was as much a part of early worship as the teaching. Paul indicates in I Corinthians 11, where he corrects the abuses that occurred during the celebration of communion at Corinth, that they gathered *for the purpose* of celebrating communion. This is why they "came together."

At Cornerstone, we practice communion at least monthly. (We do not have the space here to discuss all the reasons why we practice frequent communion. If you wish to know more about it, you may obtain the message *Why We Celebrate Communion So Often* from the church bookstore). The first Sunday of the month, we gather for *Celebration Sunday!*, and we observe the Lord's Supper together. We usually conclude the service with a fellowship meal, where we enjoy a meal together as the body of Christ and welcome anyone who can stay and eat with us. Communion is a part of worship.

The Prayers. When the church gathers for worship, we gather to pray. It is important to note that we do not merely pray *before* the service, though we do that as well. But we pray *during* the service. We are called to worship as priests before God, and as priests we offer intercession on behalf of the world.

We pray individual prayers on a daily basis; but it is important that we gather as the church, the body of Christ, to pray corporate prayers on behalf of the world. Paul, in his instruction to Timothy of how "one ought to behave in the household of God" (I Timothy 3:15), instructed Timothy to offer four types of prayer in the public worship service.

First of all, then, I urge that supplications, prayers, intercessions, and thanksgivings be made for all people, for kings and all who are in high positions, that we may lead a peaceful and quiet life, godly and dignified in every way. This is good, and it is pleasing in the sight of God our Savior, who desires all people to be saved and to come to the knowledge of the truth. For there is one God, and there is one mediator between God and men, the man Christ Jesus, who gave himself as a ransom for all, which is the testimony given at the proper time. For this I was appointed a preacher and an apostle (I am telling the truth, I am not lying), a teacher of the Gentiles in faith and truth. I desire then that in every place the men should pray, lifting holy hands without anger or quarreling; (1 Timothy 2:1-8)

The first prayer is *supplication*. As you will notice, we open every Sunday service with a prayer of supplication, usually a Psalm. Supplication entreats the Lord to hear us as we gather to worship, to forgive our sins and prepare us to minister in the holy tabernacle. Second, Paul instructs Timothy to offer "*prayers*," which seems to indicate formal, liturgical prayers, such as the prayers that Israel offered during certain seasons of worship and devotion to God according to their festal calendar. This would also include familiar prayers such as the Lord's Prayer, or Psalm 23. This is one reason why we pray the Lord's Prayer every Sunday.

The third type of prayer is *intercession*. We offer intercession each Sunday, when we pray "for kings and all who are in high positions, that we may lead a peaceful and quiet life, godly and dignified in every way" (I Timothy 2:2). We pray for our President, our Congress, our Governor, Mayor and other civic leaders. *This is what we come to church to do.* These things are not mere preliminaries to the sermon. We are called together to offer prayers in the house of God.

Finally, the fourth prayer is the prayer of *thanksgiving*, and we offer this prayer during the "Ascent to Worship" each Sunday and during the prayers that conclude the service in the benediction. The Benediction Prayer concludes with the blessing that God commanded the priests to place upon the people at the end of the assembly.

> The LORD spoke to Moses, saying, "Speak to Aaron and his sons, saying, Thus you shall bless the people of Israel: you shall say to them, The LORD bless you and keep you; the LORD make his face to shine upon you and be gracious to you; the LORD lift up his countenance upon you and give you peace. So shall they put my name upon the people of Israel, and I will bless them." (Numbers 6:22-27)

The Order of Service

At Cornerstone, our Sunday morning service follows the pattern of the sacrifices offered in the Temple, seeing that they were simply the earthly pattern of heavenly worship. We begin with a "Call to Worship," though this may be preceded with a prelude of music and singing as we gather into the sanctuary. Then, we offer "Confession of Sin" and pray "The Lord's Prayer," which concludes with an extemporaneous prayer for the congregation to be forgiven of their sins and be prepared to minister in the Holy Place. The "Call to Worship," "Confession of Sin" and "The Lord's Prayer" correspond to the trespass offerings that were presented first when the priests of Israel offered worship.

Next, we open our "worship service" (which is the general term used to describe the singing) with the "Ascent to Worship," which corresponds to the burnt offerings, or rather, the "ascension offerings," offered in the Temple. Then, we offer our praise and worship as incense unto God, as the writer of Hebrews said, "Through him then let us continually offer up a sacrifice of praise to God, that is, the fruit of lips that acknowledge his name" (Hebrews 13:15).

After singing and praising God with reverence and rejoicing, we offer up the incense of intercession, as noted above. When intercession is over, we usually "extend the peace of the Lord" through the *koinonia* of greeting our brothers and sisters in the Lord and all who may be visiting with us in the service. Then, we receive our tithes and offerings, which is a part of *koinonia* and priestly service to the Lord.

Next, we pray over the hearing of the Word and receive the preached Word. After the Word is preached, we gather around the altars for prayer and meditation on the Word. Those that wish to repent of their sins and be converted and those that desire prayer for healing or other needs are invited to come forward at this time, and the elders and ministers of the church pray for them.

Finally, we conclude the Sunday service with announcements—a *very* important part of a thriving Christian community!—and the Benediction.

CONCLUSION

We have considered two questions: first, *why* do we worship on the Lord's Day? Second, *how* do we worship on the Lord's Day? We are considering this because, at Cornerstone Church, our Sunday service may seem a little different than what some have experienced before. If they come from a Pentecostal or other "free church" background, then the Sunday service may seem a little formal for their taste. If they come from a "high church" background, this pattern of worship may seem familiar at first, but there will certainly be elements of worship that surprise them with their spontaneity and enthusiasm.

Those that come to Cornerstone without any sort of religious background may simply accept the way things are done as the way they *should* be done—yet, we want everyone to understand the way we worship so we may sing praises "with understanding" (Psalm 47:7). The main thing is that we all understand why we worship the way we do, and that we embrace it as an-ever growing understanding of the pattern for worship set forth in Scripture. It is important that we worship God the way He wants to be worshipped.

The last thing we should mention is the fundamental importance of attending worship faithfully. The Lord commands us to blow the trumpet and assemble the people before Him. When church is going on and we are absent, we are not just missing church—we are missing the assembly of the people before the Lord.

When we miss church, there is an element of contribution and participation that is lacking. When a member of the body is missing, the gifts that the Holy Spirit has distributed throughout the body within each member are not fully present. When we miss, we fail to:

WORSHIP → CONNECT → SERVE

CHAPTER THREE

WORSHIP AS A WAY OF LIFE

WORSHIP BEYOND THE BOUNDARIES

When we think of worship, we tend to think of what we do at church. However, worship is much bigger than that. Worship encompasses all of life. We were created to worship God in everything we do. Think back to creation before the fall of man. It is almost impossible to imagine a world where worship was limited to a once a week religious event on the Sabbath. It is rather obvious from the creation account in Genesis that every aspect of Adam's world was governed by his relationship with God. Indeed, all creation was formed to be the dwelling place of God's holiness (Romans 1). Adam was not created to worship God once a week and to do as he pleased the rest of the time. No, we readily understand that God created Adam to worship Him in everything, in all of life. We must do the same.

No doubt, there is a sense in which worship, properly and formally understood, refers to what we do at church. There really is a difference, for example, between celebrating communion and eating a meal at home. We have seen that already in Acts 2:42, 46. There is a spiritual aspect to worshipping at church that transcends everyday life.

However, there is another sense in which everything we do, including eating at home, is spiritual. In other words, though we recognize the uniqueness of what we do at church, we should understand that the uniqueness of what we do at church *has a profound effect on everything we do outside of church*. To put it simply, worship at church sanctifies all of life and transforms the "secular" into the sacred.

Think about it: when God chose to dwell among His people, Israel, by descending and resting upon the Mercy Seat in the Tabernacle, His presence in the Tabernacle—at *church*—sanctified the entire congregation and made them a holy community unto the Lord. This meant that they were sanctified as vessels of holiness that carried the holiness of God into all creation. They were to be holy in their diet, their attire and their behavior toward others. To be worshippers of God meant that they were to live in a different way in everything. We must do the same.

The Sacred/Secular Dichotomy

Scholars, both historians and theologians, tell us that the world has been divided into a "sacred/secular dichotomy" since the Enlightenment period of the 17th Century. Before that time, experts widely agree that people rarely, if ever, thought in terms of dividing the spiritual world from the physical world. Since the Enlightenment, this "holistic" view of life, where all is spiritual, is considered by many intellectuals to be ignorant superstition. Those that think they "know," think they know better. They consider themselves "enlightened." Paul's word comes to mind: "Professing themselves to be wise, they have become fools" (Romans 1:22).

In reality, against all its utopian dreams, however, the Enlightenment has cast long, evil shadows upon human history. It provided the philosophical basis for radical materialism, both in its capitalistic (money is god) and socialistic (government is god) forms. If God is squeezed into a once-a-week religious corner, then the rest of life loses its meaning and become purely narcissistic and self-centered. The ultimate end of self-worshipping materialism is Fascism and Communism, both of which have slaughtered their millions in the name of philanthropic human progress. Some "enlightenment."

This "secular/sacred dichotomy" has affected us more than we know. For example, in America, we are accustomed to hearing much about "the separation of church and state." In one sense, this is a noble idea—the idea that the church should not be controlled by the government and vice versa. However, in modern times, "the separation of church and state" has become "the separation of *God* and state," and that is an entirely different matter. The church may not rule the state, but God *does*.

Now, secularists have now begun pushing to exclude religious faith from the public square altogether, including work, school and play. This is unacceptable to Christians, for we believe that Jesus is Lord of all of life and everything we do is worship. At least, that is what Christians *should* believe! And, by the grace of God, that is what we *shall* believe.

In the Temple and from House to House

The early Christians believed that God rules over all of life; therefore He should be worshipped in all life. They believed that all of life is the gift of God, our life at work, at home, at school, at play, and everywhere else. Since we all "live and move and have our being" (Acts 17:28) through His sovereign providence, then we should offer Him thanks and give Him glory in everything.

Look again at Acts 2 for an example of this out-growing, ever-expanding influence of worship that begins at church and flows through the home into the world at large.

> And day by day, attending the temple together and breaking bread in their homes, they received their food with glad and generous hearts, praising God and having favor with all the people. And the Lord added to their number day by day those who were being saved. (Acts 2:46-47)

This is a great example of what I like to call "taking church home." The early church worshipped God daily in the temple, but they did not leave Him "on the pew" when they went home. They carried their devotion home with them. They "praised God" at home. They enjoyed the material pleasures of food with "glad and generous hearts, praising God." Moreover, their Spirit-filled, everyday lives affected the people in their neighborhood, where they worked and where they shopped. The early church believed that worship is all of life, and all of life is worship.

Paul integrates worship with everyday life in a powerful way in both Ephesians 5 and Colossians 3. In both passages, Paul challenges the church to live out their Christian vocation with exemplary godly behavior. Paul addresses believers as wives, husbands, parents, children, masters and slaves. And right in the middle of these exhortations, Paul teaches them to worship, to offer up "psalms, hymns and spiritual songs," which are songs that are Spirit-filled, and they are to do this *as* members of the household. As wives, husbands, parents, children, masters and slaves, they are called to worship God at all times. Paul's point, which is not limited to singing, is that we bring praise to God in everything we do.

When we think of taking worship home, we generally think of doing at home what we do at church. In other words, we think of singing at home, praying at home, rejoicing in praise at home, and so on. And, certainly, we need to fill our homes with praise and worship, with prayers and Scripture reading. Yet the point for which we are grasping here is that *all of life* is worship in a larger sense. For a carpenter that believes that "the earth is the Lord's and the fullness thereof," driving nails is worship. For the nurse that believes that healing comes from God and not from a pharmaceutical company, administering medicine is worship. And this is true in every vocation.

Of course, this does not mean that the carpenter, the nurse, or any other worker, can justify neglecting formal, corporate worship at church by claiming that they only need to worship God through their vocation. Not at all! Indeed, the point we raised earlier is that it is our worship together as the body of Christ, gathering where Jesus gathers when "two or three" assemble in His name, that sanctifies the "secular" and makes it "sacred." Working with your hands is worship only when it is done by hands that are lifted in praise every Sunday in the house of the Lord.

DAILY WORSHIP

So far, we have considered the idea that worship is more than just what we do at church. It is more than *what* we do and *where* we do it. Worship is all of life. Yet, we must not think that we can "de-spiritualize" our lives by worshipping God *only* through "secular" vocation to the neglect of praise, prayer and meditation on the Word. These things, done daily, are the means by which we keep our vocation focused. Morning devotions, for example, set the tone for the rest of the day. When we take the time to pray, to read a select passage of Scripture, and to meditate on its meaning for us for today, the work we pursue is transformed into an expression of that devotion to God.

Morning prayer sanctifies the day. Morning prayer transforms the first moments of waking into the first fruits of worship that hallows the remaining hours of the day. Through morning devotions, the carpenter, the nurse, and all others, condition their minds to see their daily tasks as incarnational expressions of the love of Christ to the world. When the Word is prayerfully considered, the Word "becomes flesh" (John 1:14) in our daily life.

Then, when a believer has started the day off with prayer, Scripture reading and meditation on the Word, he or she should maintain a spirit of worship throughout the rest of the day by carefully guarding their conversation. Not only should they avoid conversation that does not glorify God, but also they should deliberately and intentionally seek conversation that encourages worship. This can be done through emails, texting, social networking (such as Facebook, Twitter, etc), and phone calls that specifically seek to glorify God in daily conversation. Driving nails, driving a truck—or driving a golf ball, for that matter!—in Jesus' name to the glory of God is hard to do when your conversation is corrupt.

Listening to music that glorifies God is another way of making worship all of life. We are blessed these days to have music readily available to us on the radio, online, on our phones and MP3 players. We can set the tone for our day, if we choose to do so. What we listen to controls the atmosphere of our home, our work or our school. However, we must not simply listen. We cannot permit the "professionals" to do all our praising for us. We must lift up our voice and sing for ourselves. We must "speak to ourselves in psalms, hymns and spiritual songs." This is the sort of talking to yourself that is not a sign of insanity!

However we do it, we must learn to make worship all of life. There is no realm of life that escapes the Lordship of Jesus Christ. He rules over all, and we must worship Him in all.

CONCLUSION

After we learn to worship in all of life, we can expect that this worship-saturation will begin to have an effect. It will affect our families, our friends, our co-workers, and us. Most importantly, it will affect God, and He will begin to bless us abundantly as we seek first His kingdom and righteousness. The Bible teaches, and the meteorologist will confirm it, that the rain comes down where the vapor goes up (Job 36:27 KJV). In other words, if we will lift up the vapor of praise, God will pour out the rain of blessing.

Then, our life will begin to bear the fruit of God's blessing, and others will see His hand upon our life. Advancement will come as a result. Promotion, which comes from the hand of God (Psalm 75:6), will follow in every endeavor. As we see in Acts 2:46, 47, praising God daily brings favor with God and with people. The ultimate result is that "the Lord added to their number day by day those who were being saved." We shall discuss this further when we talk about "Mission." But for now, we should point out that worship as a way of life brings sinners to the way of life, the life of God in Christ manifest through the church.

CHAPTER FOUR

WORSHIP AS WAR

WHEN HEAVEN OPENS

One of the greatest moments in the life of a worshipper is when "heaven opens" and he or she sees the cosmic significance of mundane worship ("mundane" in the proper sense "of this world"). The "cosmic significance of mundane worship"—what on earth does that mean? Simply this: when we worship, there is more going on than we can see.

When we worship, heaven gets involved with earth. Or, to put it more accurately, earth gets involved with heaven. Worship occurs at the intersection of heaven and earth, at Bethel, where God meets with man, and the angels ascend and descend upon the Son of Man, Jesus Christ and the body of Christ, the church.

One of the first principles of worship that mankind learned is that there is more going on than meets the eye. The first worship service recorded in Scripture shows that heaven was intimately involved with earth when Cain and Abel presented sacrifices as worship to God. There was much more happening than animals and produce burning on an altar made of stone. Their worship invoked the involvement of heaven, and God was directly and deeply interested in the proceedings.

From the beginning God met with man on a mountain (the Garden of Eden was planted upon a mountain), which meant that man's worship ascended up to enter the heavens. From the time of Cain and Abel, the sacrificial altar was designed as a mountain-in-miniature where God would meet with man. The physical symbolism was given to represent an invisible, yet very *real,* reality: heaven and earth intersect in the worship event.

When God created the world, He drew the curtain of the firmament over "the heaven of heavens" and placed His throne behind "the veil." However, God designed worship to give a prophetic glimpse behind that veil that spoke of the day when heaven and earth would be one, and God would walk in full fellowship with man.

There are several instances in Scripture where God opened up the heavens and allowed worshippers to see what goes on beyond the veil. In these moments, the worshippers were allowed to see how the earthly worship corresponded with and reflected the worship of heaven. Isaiah 6 is an example of such a moment. The prophet Ezekiel saw heaven through an open door. Jacob saw angels ascending and descending at Bethel. One of the greatest examples of this "peek" behind the scenes at the worship of heaven is *The Book of Revelation.* Here, John ascended through an open door into the heavenlies and beheld a full-blown worship service in the heavenly temple of God. What an experience!

Yet, we share this experience every Sunday. We are lifted up into heavenly places when we worship. Paul speaks of this reality in Ephesians. He tells us that Christ has ascended into the heavens:

> I do not cease to give thanks for you, remembering you in my prayers, that the God of our Lord Jesus Christ, the Father of glory, may give you a spirit of wisdom and of revelation in the knowledge of him, having the eyes of your hearts enlightened, that you may know what is the hope to which he has called you, what are the riches of his glorious inheritance in the saints, and what is the immeasurable greatness of his power toward us who believe, according to the working of his great might that he worked in Christ when he raised him from the dead and seated him at his right hand in the heavenly places, far above all rule and authority and power and dominion, and above every name that is named, not only in this age but also in the one to come. And he put all things under his feet and gave him as head over all things to the church, which is his body, the fullness of him who fills all in all. (Ephesians 1:16-23)

Keep reading:

> And you were dead in the trespasses and sins in which you once walked, following the course of this world, following the prince of the power of the air, the spirit that is now at work in the sons of disobedience— among whom we all once lived in the passions of our flesh, carrying out the desires of the body and the mind, and were by nature children of wrath, like the rest of mankind. But God, being rich in mercy, because of the

great love with which he loved us, even when we were dead in our trespasses, made us alive together with Christ—by grace you have been saved—and raised us up with him and seated us with him in the heavenly places in Christ Jesus, so that in the coming ages he might show the immeasurable riches of his grace in kindness toward us in Christ Jesus. For by grace you have been saved through faith. And this is not your own doing; it is the gift of God, not a result of works, so that no one may boast. For we are his workmanship, created in Christ Jesus for good works, which God prepared beforehand, that we should walk in them. (Ephesians 2:1-10)

So, not only has Christ ascended into heaven to preside over the worship of the heavens as King and Priest "forever after the order of Melchizedec," but also *we* have ascended together with Christ inasmuch that our worship on the earth is aligned with His worship in the heavens. The point here is that our worship on earth must be done "on earth as it is in heaven," as the Lord's Prayer petitions. When we worship in Spirit and in truth, the Father, who seeks such to worship Him, is glorified and is enthroned upon our praise. This is what we mean when we speak of "ascending to worship."

Worship is a celebration of the lordship of Jesus, and this means that worship has a cosmic dimension that is often lost in our personal, pietistic forms of worship that reduce worship down to only "Jesus is Lord of my heart." He is Lord of more than our heart! He is Lord of all creation and that is true right now. Worship celebrates this reality.

WAR IN THE HEAVENS

There is another aspect to worshiping "in the heavenlies" that we should consider. In fact, this point is *the* point to which we are hastening. Worship is war. When we worship the one true God, all other gods resist us. Now, the gods that we are confronting are in league with Satan, "the god of this world" (II Corinthians 4:4), and they really are not gods at all. The gods that we confront are the principalities and powers that were originally created as holy angels to serve man in his dominion over the earth. These angels rebelled with Satan in the Garden of Eden and were cast out with the Serpent when he fell.

The Powers have enslaved the hearts of men by controlling the economic systems, religious systems and political systems of the world. However, Jesus defeated them at Calvary. He "disarmed the rulers and authorities and put them to open shame, by triumphing over them in him" (Colossians 2:13-15), and the "Church Militant" is now actualizing through evangelism the victory of Christ over the Powers. Worship is the central front in this war.

When we worship the one true God, we come to:

…Mount Zion and to the city of the living God, the heavenly Jerusalem, and to innumerable angels in festal gathering, and to the assembly of the firstborn who are enrolled in heaven, and to God, the judge of all, and to the spirits of the righteous made perfect, and to Jesus, the mediator of a new covenant, and to the sprinkled blood that speaks a better word than the blood of Abel. (Hebrews 12:22-24)

As we read earlier in Ephesians 2, when we worship we are "seated together" with Christ in the heavenlies. To be "seated together" means much more than just reclining on comfortable pews in a heavenly sanctuary. No, it means that we are enthroned with Christ in the heavens. To be "seated together" in heaven means *to be seated on thrones.* When we worship, we rule. Christ's *enthronement* caused the Powers' *dethronement.* And this is not only *true,* it is totally infuriating to the Powers. Satan has come down with "great wrath, because he knows that his time is short!" (Revelation 12:12) Thus, when we worship, we can expect a fight.

When we worship, we make war on three levels. We confront the Powers *personally, locally* and *globally.* In other words, we go to war against spirits that work against us as individuals; against spirits that resist the church as a worshipping body; and against spirits that bind our city, our nation and our world. When we worship, we are "casting out devils" on every level of human existence. We are proclaiming the lordship of Jesus as kings, priests and prophets.

Some Christians discern only one or two of the three levels of spiritual resistance, but we must engage the Adversary on all levels. Our worship must break through the resistance that we encounter in our own mind, in our personal struggle to magnify the Lord over every situation in our life. Our worship must break through every spiritual barrier that obstructs the church as a body from experiencing free and victorious worship as we gather each Lord's Day. And our worship must break through the entrenched opposition that the Powers exert against the advance of the church in this city and every nation under heaven. The church must preach, pray and praise its way to victory. Worship is war!

In the Old Testament, worship and war were directly connected. There are a few instances where the people of God actually worshipped as they made war, singing and playing music as the armies marched out to battle. But in the larger sense, all of Israel's worship was a direct challenge to the false gods that filled the land of Canaan. The Temple was placed at the center of the known world as a witness to the one true God and as a warning to all false gods: you must bow down before the Lord of all creation!

The Psalms of Israel show worship as directly confronting the powers of the world at large, including false gods and evil rulers. The songs that Israel sang were songs that declared the universal glory of God and the lying reproach of all pretenders. (This is one reason why we must be careful to sing the way the Bible teaches us to sing. Otherwise, our weapons of war shall surely misfire!) Israel's Psalter, which was their "hymnal," was filled with worship songs and prayers that daily reminded the people that they were in hostile territory. Yet they were reminded to never fear, for the Lord God omnipotent reigns!

The Book of Revelation is an epic example of worship as war. Too often we see *Revelation* as only a description of a terrible war on earth. But worship in heaven is at the center of the war on earth. In fact, it is worship in heaven that causes, compels and completes the war on earth. The war is fought over worship: *whom* shall we worship, the Lamb or the Beast? And the answer comes: "Worthy is the Lamb who was slain, to receive power and wealth and wisdom and might and honor and glory and blessing!"

When Paul speaks of spiritual warfare in both II Corinthians 10 and Ephesians 6, he speaks of worship: preaching (II Corinthians 10); salvation; justification; truth; sword of the Spirit, the Word of God; evangelism; and faith (Ephesians 6). Jesus connected the defeat of Satan with the preaching of the gospel (Luke 10). *Worship is war!* This is why we often encounter spiritual resistance while we worship. Churches that ascend into the heavenlies to worship *knowingly* will be aware of spiritual hindrances that would otherwise go unnoticed. We must press through to victory in worship.

CONCLUSION

Worship is central to the evangelistic ministry and mission of the church. The church is called to declare the gospel, the Good News, that Christ has risen and all creation is made new in Him. The Powers have been dethroned, and Christ and His church now rule. Of course, we know that the fullness of our rule with Christ awaits the resurrection when all things are made new. But we anticipate that future *now* as we worship.

By declaring what is coming, we make what is coming come. Worship is the catalyst of the new creation. This is why we must work to fill every nation with right worship. When the church is rightly worshipping God in every nation under heaven, all creation will resonate with the praise of the one true God. The soil, the trees, the mountains will sing together with us. When the earth is filled with the glory of the Lord, then the power of darkness cannot hold back the dawning with the rising of the Son.

Remember, worship is more than what we do on Sunday, though, certainly, Sunday anchors the center of gravity that gives balance to all our worship. But worship is all of life. So, as we worship in everything we do, we are advancing the kingdom of God in the earth. Live life in such a way that everything you do will be done in the name of Jesus to the glory of God. Then, the Powers that resist you will be defeated. The Powers that oppose our church and its growth in the earth will be defeated. And finally, the Powers that resist the advance of the rule of God in every nation will be defeated. And all of this shall be done as we worship. Come! Let us worship the Lord!

PART TWO: CONNECT

CHAPTER FIVE

CONNECTING AS THE BODY OF CHRIST

INTRODUCTION

As we continue our series on **WORSHIP → CONNECT → SERVE**, we turn our focus toward the way Christians who worship the one, true God are joined together by that worship into one coherent community of believers. We shall consider how the church *connects*.

We have discussed worship in oneness, worship on the Lord's Day, worship as a way of life, and worship as war. Now, we shall take a look at (1) how we connect as the body of Christ; (2) how we connect through koinonia (which we shall define again); (3) how we connect through the mutual benefit of the gifts of the Spirit; and (4) how we connect with the saints throughout the nations and throughout history, with all the saints in earth and in heaven.

There are three primary metaphors of the church in the New Testament Scriptures: a body, a building and a bride. Each of these convey different aspects of the church and its relation to God and to fellow believers, but each one centers on the idea of "connection." A body is connected, made up of many parts; a building is connected, made of many stones and beams; and a bride is connected in marital relations with her husband.

Though the idea of being the bride of Christ and, especially, of being the building of God, His holy temple, are never far from the back of our mind as we work our way through these lessons, the primary metaphor we shall use in the next four lessons on "connecting" is the *body* of Christ. This is the image that Paul the apostle uses the most, and we shall follow a good deal of his teaching as we go along. Let's get started!

THE CHURCH AS THE BODY OF CHRIST

Before we get started talking about the church and how it connects as a worshipping community, we should probably define what the church is. After two thousand years of Christian history it would be easy to take for granted that everyone knows what "church" means. However, there is a great deal of confusion about the meaning of "church," even among Christians. We do not have space here for a good discussion of ecclesiology (the doctrine of the church), but we should at least define the word "church."

The word "church" comes from the Greek word *ekklesia*. Though this word has come to be identified with the Christian community, it was originally a rather generic Greek word that was used to describe the civic assembly of any particular community in the Greek world. *Ekklesia* simply means "called out to come together." The word gained its association with the worshipping community when the Jewish Rabbis chose this word to translate the Hebrew word for "congregation" in Old Testament Scriptures as they prepared the Septuagint (the ancient Greek version of the Old Testament). The church is simply the congregation of God's people "called out to come together."

The idea of the church as the body of Christ is an idea that flows out of the Old Covenant idea of Israel as the "body of Moses." Jude speaks of Michael contending for the "body of Moses" (Jude 9), which seems to be a clear reference to the cosmic struggle over the nation of Israel in Zechariah 3. The metaphors mentioned above of the people of God as God's bride and God's building are also first found in the Old Testament in reference to Israel. However, the point of the church as "the body of Christ" is that the church is assembled together as one community made of many members. It is the idea of being *connected* that is illustrated here.

THE INDIVIDUAL AND COMMUNAL BODY OF CHRIST

The body of Christ is both the individual man, Christ Jesus, and the company of believers that are joined together in His name by His indwelling Spirit. This "both-and" is very important. There are professing Christians that claim to be the body of Christ but they do not believe in the present existence in resurrected glory of the actual man, Christ Jesus. They deny the actual, physical resurrection of Jesus. They reduce the church down to just the visible Christian community. However, if Christ is not raised from the dead and existing in bodily form in the heavens pouring forth His Spirit into believers, then there is no spiritual and existential basis for the coherent community of believers. Without Christ, there is no body of Christ.

On the other hand, there are professing believers that claim to be joined to Christ but they deny the church, the community of faith that is built up in Christ by His indwelling Spirit. They believe that they can be a part of the body of Christ without associating with the visible church, the formal gathering of the Christian community. They may marshal a thousand arguments for why they do not need the church, but the stubborn fact remains: you cannot be in fellowship with the Christ without being baptized into His church and gathering together with the church to worship the one true God in spirit and truth.

The writer of Hebrews exhorts faltering believers to be faithful to attend church, especially when times of hardship and trouble press in upon the church.

Let us hold fast the confession of our hope without wavering, for he who promised is faithful. And let us consider how to stir up one another to love and good works, *not neglecting to meet together*, as is the habit of some, but encouraging one another, and all the more as you see the Day drawing near. For if we go on sinning deliberately after receiving the knowledge of the truth, there no longer remains a sacrifice for sins, but a fearful expectation of judgment, and a fury of fire that will consume the adversaries. Anyone who has set aside the Law of Moses dies without mercy on the evidence of two or three witnesses. How much worse punishment, do you think, will be deserved by the one who has spurned the Son of God, and has profaned the blood of the covenant by which he was sanctified, and has outraged the Spirit of grace? For we know him who said, "Vengeance is mine; I will repay." And again, "The Lord will judge his people." It is a fearful thing to fall into the hands of the living God. (Hebrews 10:23-31; emphasis added)

These are strong words, and they are spoken to those that are tempted to believe that they can be a part of the "invisible church" without being a part of the "visible church." It simply is not possible.

Of course, there are times when people are unable to physically attend worship gatherings because they are sick, imprisoned or other unavoidable circumstances. Yet, even in these circumstances the church is taught to "remember" those that cannot attend and gather them together with the church by the Spirit through prayer. Look at Hebrews again:

> Remember those who are in prison, as though in prison with them, and those who are mistreated, since you also are in the body. (Hebrews 13:3)

We are to "remember those who are in prison" because we "also are in the body." Because we are all members of the body of Christ we should gather into our worship by the Spirit even those who are absent through no fault of their own. We shall consider this further below.

THE BODY OF CHRIST AS THE IMAGE OF GOD

The body of Christ—both Christ and the church—exists as the image of God to show forth the universal expression of the invisible God. Christ is the visible image of God the Father. However, God's infinite glory is fully expressed in the church, "which is his body, the fullness of him who fills all in all" (Ephesians 1:22-23). God's fullness flows through Christ into the church by the indwelling power of the Holy Spirit, Who mediates the presence and power of Christ into all nations through individual believers. This means that the *full* fullness of God can only be seen in the church.

Paul says,

> To me, though I am the very least of all the saints, this grace was given, to preach to the Gentiles the unsearchable riches of Christ, and to bring to light for everyone what is the plan of the mystery hidden for ages in God who created all things, so that *through the church* the manifold wisdom of God might now be made known to the rulers and authorities in the heavenly places. (Ephesians 3:8-10; emphasis added)

The "manifold" (multifaceted) wisdom of God cannot be fully manifest apart from the church. When the church is fully built up in all *space* (throughout the heavens and earth) and *time* (throughout history), then, and only then, will the fullness of God's glory be manifest. And even *then*, the church will continue to grow in the image and glory of God for eternity, ever increasing in its manifestation of the manifold wisdom of God. It takes an always expanding universe and a never-ending eternity to fully reveal the glory of God.

God created Adam to be His image and likeness, but it is evident that Adam alone could not fully display the radiance of God's glory. This is why Christ Jesus came to die for a new human race that would be born again and filled with the Spirit of God. It is Christ's glory to be glorified in the unity and diversity of the church, which is His body.

Christ fully expresses the image of God as He is glorified in the church. Christ's spirit flows out into believers, and He is omnipresenced in the church. This is the "joy that was set before Him" (Hebrews 12:2; cf. Psalm 16:11), that He might experience the existential fullness of being that only comes when a man flows out of himself and finds fulfillment in the fullness of others.

Moreover, this is our destiny: to be glorified with Christ and to be filled with the Spirit in such a way that we flow out of ourselves into one another and contribute to each other's existential fullness. There is revelation here of the oneness of God and the oneness of His people that only eternity can fully disclose. There is a revelation here of relationship, of how we *connect*.

BUILDING THE CHURCH

Matthew 16

Jesus came to build His church. He promised that He would build His church upon the rock of the revelation of who He is and the relationship that proceeds from that revelation.

> Now when Jesus came into the district of Caesarea Philippi, he asked his disciples, "Who do people say that the Son of Man is?" And they said, "Some say John the Baptist, others say Elijah, and others Jeremiah or one of the prophets." He said to them, "But who do you say that I am?" Simon Peter replied, "You are the Christ, the Son of the living God." And Jesus answered him, "Blessed are you, Simon Bar-Jonah! For flesh and blood has not revealed this to you, but my Father who is in heaven. And I tell you, you are Peter, and on this rock I will build my

church, and the gates of hell shall not prevail against it. I will give you the keys of the kingdom of heaven, and whatever you bind on earth shall be bound in heaven, and whatever you loose on earth shall be loosed in heaven." Then he strictly charged the disciples to tell no one that he was the Christ. (Matthew 16:13-20)

It is pretty obvious that Jesus plans to build His church on the revelation and confession of who He is. But there is something more here. Jesus responded to Peter's confession of faith by declaring who *Peter* was: "And I tell you, you are Peter," which was a statement of reciprocal *relationship* between Jesus and Peter. Then, Jesus goes on to show how Peter's relationship with Him would flow out into a mutual relationship with Peter and his brethren. The revelation of Christ leads to the revelation of the church.

Look at it closer. First, Jesus made a subtle play on words using Peter's name, which means, "rock." Though there is no doubt that many have misused this idea to promote a false idea of papal succession, there is still some truth to the idea that Jesus referred to Peter as "a rock" upon which the church would be built. Peter later told us that we *all* are living stones of which the temple of God is built (I Peter 2:5). The revelation-relationship of Jesus Christ is the foundation stone upon which Peter and all other believers are placed as the living stones that build up the temple.

Second, Jesus told Peter that he would be given the keys to the kingdom, which means that Peter and his brethren, the disciples, would have the authority to "bind and loose" on earth what is "bound and loosed in heaven." To "bind and loose" is to have the authority to rule as officers and elders of the Christian community. Peter and the apostles were given the "keys of the kingdom of heaven," which meant that they had the power open and shut the gates of heaven, as the elders of a community in Jesus' time would have done for their city. It also meant that the apostles, as the elders of the City of God, would have the power to record or blot out names written on the citizen's roll. In another place, Jesus called this the power to "remit" and "retain" sins (John 20:23 KJV).

This means, quite simply, that the church is built on more than just a revelation of who Jesus is. The church is built on a revelation of who *the church* is. The church is built on a revelation of relationship—or, to put it more exactly, a *revelation-relationship,* a revelation that flows out into relationship, and a relationship that creates deeper revelation. The church is built upon this cycle of revelation-relationship that increases with greater fullness as it grows.

Though we do not have space here to address it, there are actually three revelation-relationships in Matthew 16: (1) the revelation-relationship of Christ (vs. 13-17); (2) the revelation-relationship of the church (vs. 18-20); and (3) the revelation-relationship of the cross (vs. 21-28). It is interesting to see how these three revelation-relationships fit with the pattern of our studies here on **WORSHIP** → **CONNECT** → **SERVE.** The revelation-relationship of Christ is all about *worship.* The revelation-relationship of the church is all about *connecting.* The revelation-relationship of the cross is all about *serving* others.

Ephesians 4

The biblical doctrine of the church (which is called *ecclesiology*) is set out most clearly and comprehensively in Paul's beautiful letter to the church at Ephesus. Paul traces the predestined history and destiny of the church in chapters 1-3, and shows how this epic vision is worked out in practical terms in the latter part of chapter 4 to the end of the book in chapter 6.

But right in the middle of it all, Paul gives us a magnificent glimpse into the way the church is built and what we should expect to see *as* the church and *when* the church is built. This brilliant excursus is found in Ephesians 4:1-16. It is a somewhat lengthy selection, but it is worth reading again, slowly.

I therefore, a prisoner for the Lord, urge you to walk in a manner worthy of the calling to which you have been called, (2) with all humility and gentleness, with patience, bearing with one another in love, (3) eager to maintain the unity of the Spirit in the bond of peace. (4) There is one body and one Spirit—just as you were called to the one hope that belongs to your call— (5) one Lord, one faith, one baptism, (6) one God and Father of all, who is over all and through all and in all. (7) But grace was given to each one of us according to the measure of Christ's gift. (8) Therefore it says, "When he ascended on high he led a host of captives, and he gave gifts to men." (9) (In saying, "He ascended," what does it mean but that he had also descended into the lower parts of the earth? (10) He who descended is the one who also ascended far above all the heavens, that he might fill all things.) (11) And he gave the apostles, the prophets, the evangelists, the pastors and teachers, (12) to equip the saints for the work of ministry, for building up the body of Christ, (13) until we all attain to the unity of the faith and of the knowledge of the Son of God, to mature manhood, to the measure of the stature of the fullness of Christ, (14) so that we may no longer be children, tossed to and fro by the waves and carried about by every wind of doctrine, by human cunning, by craftiness in deceitful schemes. (15) Rather, speaking the truth in love, we are to grow up in every way into him who is the head, into Christ, (16) from whom the whole body, joined and held together by every joint with which it is equipped, when each part is working properly, makes the body grow so that it builds itself up in love. (Ephesians 4:1-16)

There is so much here that it would require volumes to discuss it fully. But the principal point that I wish to highlight is that the church is built up through *connecting*. Jesus Christ "ascended on high, He led a host of captives, and He gave gifts to men." He did this that "He might fill all things." Or, literally, that He might "fulfill the universe." And the means of bringing the universe to its intended destiny of perfect fulfillment in oneness with God is the spiritual distribution of gifts throughout the body of Christ. And this distribution only occurs when the body is properly connected.

Look at it closely. "And he gave the apostles, the prophets, the evangelists, the pastors and teachers, to equip the saints for the work of ministry, for building up the body of Christ, until we all attain to the unity of the faith and of the knowledge of the Son of God, to mature manhood, to the measure of the stature of the fullness of Christ…" The body of Christ is built up as Christ sends forth His Spirit from heaven to give gifts unto men (and to give men as gifts: both meanings are correct). Gifts of apostles, prophets, evangelists, pastors (shepherds) and teachers are given (v. 11) so that the church may be equipped for the work of service that the church may be built up (v. 12). This is how the body is built up in love (v. 16).

Again, there is a pattern here of **WORSHIP** → **CONNECT** → **SERVE**. The ascended Christ is exalted and worshipped in heaven and earth. He flows out to those who worship Him as the indwelling, gifting Holy Spirit. The Holy Spirit binds believers together in "the unity of the Spirit" (v. 3), and the church is *connected* when the "whole body, joined and held together by every joint with which it is equipped, when each part is working properly, makes the body grow so that it builds itself up in love" (v. 16). When the church is properly worshipping the exalted Christ, and the Spirit of Christ is binding the people of God together into one body, then the saints are equipped for service, "for the work of ministry" (v. 12), and the body of Christ grows into the fullness of God in Christ through the Holy Spirit.

All of this centers on the connectedness of the body of Christ. All of the giftedness in the universe cannot flow properly to the body and to the world if the members of the body are divided and scattered. They must be brought into perfect alignment and rhythm with Christ and with the church through the oneness of the Spirit.

Colossians 2

Paul speaks more about this alignment and rhythm in his letter to the church at Colossae. Paul's statement to the Colossians about the headship of Christ is one of the clearest statements in his writings about the idea of spiritual alignment:

> Let no one disqualify you, insisting on asceticism and worship of angels, going on in detail about visions, puffed up without reason by his sensuous mind, and not holding fast to the Head, from whom the whole body, nourished and knit together through its joints and ligaments, grows with a growth that is from God. (Colossians 2:18-19)

Paul shows us here that spiritual growth flows both *vertically* (growth flows from "the Head") and *horizontally* (growth flows through the body as it is "nourished and knit together"). This idea of both vertical and horizontal growth will be very important in our lesson on koinonia, where we shall discuss how we are filled with the Spirit both as it flows from God in heaven and as it flows from our brothers and sisters throughout the body. There is both a vertical and horizontal flow to the Spirit. Think of it like the rain that falls (vertical) and the river that flows (horizontal). Both bring water to parched land.

However, the point in Colossians 2 is that the church cannot grow spiritually if there is not proper alignment between Christians-and-Christ and Christians-and-the-church. Worship that is properly aligned with Christ will always bend us toward proper alignment with fellow believers.

The "growth that is from God" is a growth that comes from Christ, but it is mediated through the joints and ligaments. And *that*, my friend, is a metaphor for the person seated on the other end of your pew. Joints and ligaments is a metaphorical way of describing the relationships that are formed between fellow members of the body of Christ. Growth comes *from* the Head, which is Christ, but it flows *through* the joints and ligaments, which is our relationship with our brothers and sisters.

We cannot have a "personal relationship" with Jesus Christ—at least not a *purely* personal relationship with Jesus Christ. Our relationship with Jesus flows through our relationship with our brothers and sisters. Fullness in Christ only comes through fullness in the body of Christ. Those that profess to be aligned with Jesus but live out of sync with the body of Jesus are only fooling themselves.

The apostle John speaks along these lines in his first epistle to the church. He said,

> If anyone says, "I love God," and hates his brother, he is a liar; for he who does not love his brother whom he has seen cannot love God whom he has not seen. (1 John 4:20)

Certainly John is speaking here about loving an individual brother. But the plural surely works as well. John speaks elsewhere of loving "the brethren." So, a corporate application works perfectly here: "He who does not love *the church* whom he has seen cannot love God whom he has not seen."

There are many that profess to love God, but they have no tolerance for the church. They say they love God, but they hate Sunday School. They say they love God, but they hate fellowship dinners and *agape* meals. They say they love God, but they hate youth activities. They say they love God, but they hate attending worship on a Sunday morning. They say they love God, but they hate the people of God. On and on it goes. But this is impossible, John says. How can you say you love God, but you hate your brother? No way it can be done!

Some people love to love God because He is invisible and abstract. Moreover, they can make God to be whatever they want Him to be (they think!), while the church is more stubborn, intractable, and refuses to let them have their way and become merely a pale reflection of their every wish. They dislike the church because the church demands that they change.

But they love God—at least, the god they call their god, which is really "self"—because they can speak for Him and justify their self-will. The church is too tangible, too real, too immovable. The church refuses to bend, so they rush off in a huff and declare that they shall serve the Lord all by themselves. Sorry! You cannot love God enough to serve Him if you do not love the church enough to serve *her*.

CONCLUSION

We shall speak more about these things as we move through our next three lessons on "Connect." For now, simply grasp this point: you cannot follow Christ unless you are willing to follow the body of Christ. You cannot have Jesus without the church. You were not baptized into only a personal relationship with Jesus Christ. You were baptized by one Spirit into one body.

Trying to serve God all by yourself is like trying to play football all by yourself. It simply cannot be done. Whatever you are playing, it is *not* football. And whatever it is that you are alone, it is not a Christian. You cannot be a Christian by yourself. You cannot be a son without a father. You cannot be a wife without a husband. There are simply some relational realities that you cannot experience alone. Just so: you cannot be a Christian without the body of Christ. We need one another in order to be ourselves. We must "connect" to worship and serve. It all flows together as we

WORSHIP → CONNECT → SERVE.

CHAPTER SIX

CONNECTING THROUGH KOINONIA

INTRODUCTION

As we continue in our discussion of how the church "connects" as the body of Christ, let's consider the koinonia of the body. The word "koinonia" is an English transliteration of a Greek word that means, loosely, "fellowship" or "society." However, the word is packed with meaning, and it goes beyond merely describing a club or group. The meaning of koinonia includes the essential idea of "mutual care."

In New Testament times, "koinonia" was provided by various societies or fellowships, even laborers' guilds, that were formed to provide social interaction and mutual care for their members. Such fellowships guaranteed their members that they would be cared for in times of sickness and receive proper burial at their death. Moreover, their wives and children would be cared for after their passing. Remember, this was long before Social Security, workers' pensions and

401k's. The only support that many laborers had was their "koinonia."

When the writers of the New Testament chose to speak about the daily fellowship of early Christians, they described it as "koinonia." As we saw earlier in Acts 2:42, the early church practiced koinonia when they assembled for worship. This means that the early church saw itself as more than just a gathering that assembled to worship in one location. Rather, they saw themselves as a "mutual care society" that came together to look out for one another. They ministered to each other, encouraged one another, and helped each other make it through times of intense persecution. They sang together, prayed together, ate together, laughed and enjoyed good times together.

The early Christians also supported one another financially in times of need (Acts 2:45). This is one of the primary aspects of koinonia. They cared for their widows and orphans (Acts 6:1-7; I Timothy 5:3-16; James 1:27). They supported their ministers that gave themselves full-time to the Word and prayer (Acts 6:2; Galatians 6:6; I Corinthians 9:1-14; I Timothy 5:17, 18). And they sent out mission offerings to help distant congregations that needed financial assistance in times of distress (I Corinthians 16:1-4; II Corinthians 9). All of this is central to the idea of koinonia. It is much more than just what we tend to think of when we speak of enjoying "fellowship."

The early church believed that they were called together to look out for one another, to share mutual concern and care for one another. When you love someone, you ask about them, you check up on them, you show concern that goes beyond mere interest. When you love someone, you get involved in their needs, you become vested in their interests, and you work to help them work their problems out. You "bear one another's burdens" (Galatians 6:2). You "look not only to [your] own interests, but also to the interests of others" (Philippians 2:4). This is koinonia.

In New Testament times, no one had medical insurance. So, the church cared for its own sick. No one had burial policies, so the church helped pay for the burial of its poor. No one had food stamps or welfare, so the church fed its hungry, clothed its naked, and housed its homeless. They also did this for those outside the church. Paul said, "So then, as we have opportunity, let us do good to everyone, and especially to those who are of the household of faith" (Galatians 6:10). Benevolence was outreach to the early church.

Of course, Paul later clarifies the church's benevolence policy and states that the church should not be burdened when there are family members to meet the need (I Timothy 5:3-16). So, the family should be the first line of defense against poverty, sickness and death. Then, the church should step in when there is no one in the family able to help.

However, idolatrous government has displaced both the family and the church today. The government meets the needs of its people. No wonder government thinks that the church and the family have no say in the lives of its citizens: the government foots the bill. He who pays the fiddler calls the tune. The church was once the hands and feet of God to the world; but these days, when government has become the god of this world, the needy look to government and social benefits to meet their need. These days we pray, "Our government shall supply all our needs according to its riches in Washington." Praise be to Washington!

(By the way, this is not a thoughtless sidetrack into political theory. This is fundamental to the coming of the kingdom of God. We have no more time here to talk about it, but the family and the church must step up and fulfill their obligations to their own needy. No doubt, Christian government should help the poor, but only after the family and the church have done their part. More on that another time.)

The main point here in our introduction to koinonia is that "fellowship" in the New Testament is a much bigger concept than just getting together socially. To fellowship means to *Connect*. It means to show mutual concern and mutual care for one another whatever the need may be. We are connected. Whatever happens to you happens to me. We are in this thing together!

KOINONIA AND BAPTISM

Baptismal Initiation

To be a part of the koinonia of the church is to become a member of a covenant community. We cannot become a part of the koinonia of the church simply by attending Sunday services. We must be initiated into the covenant community. When we join the koinonia of this covenant community, we join under solemn vows to be a faithful member. Joining the church is like joining the military. We become a part of larger group seeking a larger good.

Too many these days have been fooled by the openness of the "free-church tradition" and think that church is a self-service, self-centered operation. They are wrong. The church is the body of Christ, the community of the redeemed that proclaims the lordship of Christ over all of life. The Christian church is found wherever Christ is truly communicated through the Holy Spirit in the true preaching of the gospel, the faithful practice of the sacraments (baptism and communion) and proper discipline of godly Christian living. To become a member of the church is to pledge our loyalty to Christ and to His body, the church. Koinonia is a covenant.

Every biblical covenant has an *initiation* ritual. The Christian covenant, which is called "The New Covenant," was initiated when Jesus died on the cross. This New Covenant was confirmed and Christ was vindicated when God raised Him from the dead. However, this corporate covenant must be individually activated. We must become a part of the New Covenant *personally.* We personally are initiated into the New Covenant through baptism, which is preceded by repentance and confirmed by Holy Spirit infilling. This is water and Spirit baptism.

When we are baptized, we confess that Jesus is Lord. We make a public confession of our loyalty to Him and to His church. We are joined to the local church that baptizes us, and we are joined to the universal body of Christ. The name of Jesus is invoked upon us, and we become His treasured possession. "For by one Spirit are we all baptized into one body, whether we be Jews or Gentiles, whether we be bond or free; and have been all made to drink into one Spirit" (I Corinthians 12:13). We are joined to Christ and we are joined to our brothers and sisters in Christ. When we are baptized, we become a part of the family of God, "of whom the whole family in heaven and earth is named" (Ephesians 3:15 KJV).

In water baptism, we are ordained as kings and priests. Just as Jesus was ordained to be king and priest in His baptism by John in Jordan, so we are ordained to be kings and priests when we are baptized in water and Spirit. We are washed with pure water and consecrated by the anointing oil of the Holy Spirit. When we come up from the water and stand praying (as Jesus did), the Spirit descends like a dove and the voice of the Father declares that we are His sons and daughters.

As Paul said,

> For all who are led by the Spirit of God are sons of God. For you did not receive the spirit of slavery to fall back into fear, but you have received the Spirit of adoption as sons, by whom we cry, "Abba! Father!" The Spirit himself bears witness with our spirit that we are children of God, (Romans 8:14-16)

Paul draws a direct line here between our baptism and infilling of the Spirit and the baptism of Jesus in Luke 4. (Note the parallel between the witness of the Spirit and being "led by the Spirit" in both Luke 4 and Romans 8.) However, the primary point here is that we are initiated into the covenant of a kingly and priestly community. Baptism is initiation.

Baptismal Identification

When we are initiated into the covenant community through baptism, we are also *identified* with Christ and His church. When Jesus was baptized by John in the Jordan River, it was a bold, subversive statement of *identification* with the counter-temple movement that John was leading. John, who was a priest—no doubt, considered a rogue priest by the religious establishment in Jerusalem—effectively declared that remission of sins could no longer be found in the corrupt sacrificial system preserved by the priestly Sadducean regime in Jerusalem.

John preached that forgiveness of sins could only be received by those coming out from Israel's apostasy to emerge as a baptized, holy remnant following the coming Messiah, Jesus Christ. When John saw Jesus coming to be baptized, he cried out, "Behold, the Lamb of God, who takes away the sins of the world." Jesus was baptized as an exemplar into the renewed community of Israel who came to John repenting of their sins. Jesus identified Himself with His people through baptism.

When we are baptized, we are identified with Christ and with His church, the body of Christ. Baptism assures us of a new identity as the sons and daughters of God and duly authorizes us to do the King's business.

In Matthew 28:18-20, Jesus explicitly connects authority with baptism. He said,

> And Jesus came and said to them, "All authority in heaven and on earth has been given to me. Go therefore and make disciples of all nations, baptizing them in the name of the Father and of the Son and of the Holy Spirit, teaching them to observe all that I have commanded you. And behold, I am with you always, to the end of the age." (Matthew 28:18-20)

When we are baptized, we are authorized to serve as kings and priests in the earth, and we are authorized to disciple others as they join our covenant community. We are joined together in Christian identity through Christian baptism.

Baptismal Integration

When we are baptized, we are also *integrated* into the body of Christ. Now, this is somewhat more than being initiated into or identified with the body of Christ. To be *integrated* into the body of Christ through baptism means that a process of oneness, a process of *union-through-communion*, is set in motion in baptism that does more than merely join us to the church. It actualizes our union with Christ and the church until we begin to exist as one with Christ and the church.

In other words, the life of Christ in the church begins to flow into our life until we become one existentially with the church. When this process begins, it slowly transforms us until we cannot be who we really are apart from our existence within the body of Christ. The life of the church flows into our spirit, and we are assimilated into the body, and the body is assimilated into us.

Now, it is important here to note that assimilation into the body does not mean annihilation within the body. When the life of Christ begins to flow through the church into our life, and our life is transformed into a new self in Christ, our personality is not obliterated and lost. By no means! Rather, when the life of Christ flows through the church into our life, we come alive! The person that we really are, the person we were created to become, is regenerated by the new life that now flows in us and we become more of who we are, not less. As Jesus said, we find our life by losing it in Him.

It is important to understand this point, lest we think that integration into the body means losing our individuality. Not at all! God prizes individuality. Remember what we discussed in our last lesson: the fullness of God's glory is revealed through the unity-in-diversity of the multifaceted expression of God's wisdom in the church. In other words, God is not glorified in the blandness of uniformity. God is glorified in infinite diversity.

God glories in who you are as an individual. However, who you are as an individual requires development and cultivation *that only comes through Spirit-filled communion!* God commands you to be who you are, but you cannot obey that command alone. There are aspects of your personality that cannot flourish without an "eco-system" of broad-based, diverse relationships. Cooperation and communion are essential to personal development. No other way possible!

We become who we are through integration and connection. Self-actualization cannot occur in isolation. This is the fundamental idea to our lessons on *Connect*. Baptism sets this integration in motion when you are "by one Spirit baptized into one body." Covenantal solidarity is formed when we are plunged into the body of Christ by the Spirit.

Baptismal *initiation, identification* and *integration* sets covenantal solidarity in motion. But the laws of God's creation demand that motion must be maintained or it will slowly and eventually die. Our next section shows us how the covenantal solidarity that is set in motion through baptism is kept in motion through communion.

KOINONIA AND COMMUNION

The Lord's Supper

The union-through-communion that is set in motion in baptism is kept in motion by the covenant-renewal meal of the Lord's Supper, which is also called "Communion." Now, it is obvious from Acts 2:42 that the Lord's Supper and koinonia are distinct actions of the church. Communion, properly understood, is not a subset of koinonia. Communion stands on its own as a ministry function of the church.

However, koinonia and Communion are interrelated and exist together. Communion illustrates and activates koinonia. Koinonia lives out the realities of Communion. Communion without koinonia is an "unworthy" observance of the Lord's Supper of the kind that got Corinth in so much trouble (I Corinthians 11:17-34). Both Communion and koinonia are integral to the other and cannot be properly performed without the other.

Proper Communion symbolizes and enacts the *ordinary* communion within koinonia. Learn that distinction: *proper Communion* and *ordinary communion*. Both are essential. (In this section, proper Communion is capitalized to show the distinction.)

The Lord's Supper is a covenant-renewal meal. Biblical history is replete with examples of covenant-renewal meals, and Jesus made it plain at the Last Supper that Communion was the meal of the New Covenant. The covenant is initiated when we are baptized, but it must be renewed often. When we receive Communion, we are celebrating our oneness with Christ and His body.

In fact, we are doing more than merely celebrating our oneness with Christ and His church; we are *communicating* it. We communicate our oneness in one sense by proclaiming it. But we also communicate our oneness in another sense by sharing it through the Spirit. Communion is *communicable*. We understand that Communion works, that it *does something.* Communion produces the communion that Communion celebrates.

We cannot accept the idea that Communion is a mere memorial. A memorial, yes, but not a *mere* memorial. We must insist that Communion is a memorial in the biblical sense of remembering, which means to *reenact* an event in a covenantal sense insomuch that the partakers actually relive for themselves the moment being recalled.

In this way, Christian communicants can be said to actually share in the death and resurrection of Jesus through celebrating Communion. Moreover, since we are all sharing Communion together, the reality of what happened at the Cross flows into us all by the Spirit, and we are bound together in a renewal of the covenant. Of course, Jesus does not die again. He died once for all. But *we* experience His death and resurrection again and again as we partake of the Lord's Supper.

The Holy Spirit makes Communion work. The Holy Spirit communicates the oneness of God in Christ through the Spirit into the church every time we eat the Lord's Supper. The Holy Spirit makes us one. There is no magic in the bread or the cup. The "magic" is in the power of the Holy Spirit to bring union-though-communion.

However, it is never enough just to eat the meal and then expect oneness to happen automatically. No, the oneness of the meal must be lived out. The Lord's Supper becomes a bare symbol—indeed, a mockery of true Communion—if we eat the meal and then persist in dividing the body. This is what Paul rebukes so soundly in his first letter to the Corinthians. After the meal is finished, we must live out the reality activated in the meal. Learn this: Communion must produce communion.

Communion through Communication

Consider this again: koinonia requires union-through-communion. We noted above that Communion communicates communion. That is, the Lord's Supper produces a communion that flows throughout the body as spiritual oneness. But there is another way that Communion communicates. The communion that Communion communicates requires communication. Now, *that* sounds convoluted, to say the least! But the point is really very simple. The communion that lies at the heart of koinonia is a communion that flourishes largely through talking with one another. Communion grows through conversation.

If we intend to become one with one another, we must talk to one another. Not necessarily about anything in particular, though, of course, we need to speak about things that edify. But just simple conversation has the power to join people together.

Studies have shown that two bodies will sync biologically through nothing more than a few minutes of conversation. Of course, we know that people are more than bodies, and when two people join in conversation, they open up their spirits to one another. Communion is spiritual, and we are as much spirits as we are bodies. Conversation facilitates communion.

This is why Paul spends so much time teaching on how we speak to one another. The unity of the church depends largely on how we talk to each other. It really should not be a mystery. God divided Babel by confusing their tongues, and the disunity of Babel was reversed at Pentecost when the Holy Spirit gave utterance to new tongues. But it is a travesty and mockery of the Pentecostal experience to speak in tongues like an angel at church and speak in English like the devil everywhere else. How we communicate through conversation has everything to do with how we connect as the body of Christ.

KOINONIA AND FINANCIAL RESPONSIBILITY

One final thing about koinonia. Koinonia involves covenantal financial responsibility. We spoke some about this point in the introduction above, but it must be emphasized. When you join in covenant with the church, you are pledging that you will share in the financial responsibility of covenant membership. Both Jesus and the apostles spoke often about the financial obligations of the New Covenant. We must understand the importance of our financial commitment.

There are three primary areas of financial commitment within the New Covenant community, the church: tithes, offerings, and almsgiving. We shall briefly consider each one.

Tithes

The tithe is a tenth of our financial increase that God has hallowed to Himself as a holy portion to be given in support of His priesthood and temple within the earth. The first recorded instance of a tithe being offered to God is in Genesis 14 where Abram paid tithes to Melchizedec, who was king and priest of the city of Salem. The priesthood of Melchizedec is later called "The Order of Melchizedec."

The Order of Melchizedec differs from other priesthoods in the Bible in that it is not determined by natural genealogy or lifespan but by spiritual calling (Hebrews 7). In other words, priests within the Order of Melchizedec are priests by divine appointment and not because they inherited the office from their father. Only three men have occupied this office, Melchizedec, David and Jesus (Psalm 110; Hebrews 7). Jesus now "ever lives to make intercession after the order of Melchizedec."

When Abram paid tithes to Melchizedec, he acknowledged and sanctioned a divine pattern of giving that we still follow to this day. When the Levitical priesthood was ordained under the Law of Moses, the tithe was temporarily given to the Levites and the sons of Aaron, the High Priest. When Christ came, the Levitical priesthood was "disannulled" (Hebrews 7:18), and the eternal priesthood of Christ after the Order of Melchizedec came into its fullness. The tithe that was first paid by Abram within the Order of Melchizedec has now been returned to Christ. The tithe never belonged to Moses, Levi or Aaron. They simply borrowed it until the time of Christ's fullness should come.

The simple basis for tithing in the New Covenant is this: both Genesis 14 and Hebrews 7 show that tithing belongs to the Order of Melchizedec. The church of Jesus Christ ministers in the earth as kings and priests within the Order of Melchizedec, and this is what authorizes our ministry in God's holy temple. We are not kings and priests by natural genealogy, but by spiritual calling. The church is God's priesthood and God's temple after the Order of Melchizedec. Thus, the tithe belongs to the church.

There are three aspects of tithing that directly relate to **WORSHIP → CONNECT → SERVE.** Let's look at them.

Worship. First, tithing is priestly, and we tithe as a matter of worship before God. When we bring the tenth to God, we do so as priests offering the tithe of His people in His holy temple. Everywhere tithing is portrayed or discussed in Scripture, it is set in a priestly context. Tithing is worship.

When we tithe, we hallow the money that is brought to the house of God just as the priests in the Temple hallowed the sacrifices that were brought to God. When something is hallowed to God, the common is made sacred. Money is hallowed when we tithe. Since the Fall of Adam, money has been tainted by the greed that drives men to seek after money more than anything else. The Bible calls money "filthy lucre" and "unrighteous mammon." Money is corrupt through greed, and tithing breaks the power of that corruption and sanctifies money to the purpose of God. The only way to break the power of money is to give it away.

Jesus described money as God greatest adversary: "No man can serve two masters; you must either serve God or money" (Matthew 6:24). Now, *that* is a surprising statement. We would expect Jesus to describe God's greatest opponent as Satan, or the devil, but He does not. He indicates that money is the other god that most often ensnares the allegiance of man.

So, money must be sanctified, and sanctification is a priestly task. In other words, our money can only be made holy through the ministry of a holy priesthood. Tithing sanctifies our money.

Moreover, priestly ministry is *representative*—the part represents the whole. The offering of firstfruits to God is a great example of this representative principle. As Paul said to the church at Rome, when the firstfruit is holy, the lump is holy. Tithing works just like this. When we give God the tenth of our increase, we are actually giving all we own. By giving God the priestly portion, we sanctify the remainder. When we tithe, we give all we own to the Lord.

Connect. Second, tithing is more than an offering of worship to the Lord. Tithing is also something we do in solidarity with other believers. Tithing is covenantal, and tithing is a matter of loyalty to God and the church. When we tithe, we play our part on the "team." When we tithe, *we enter into covenant with God* that He shall be Lord of all our finance, that He will be our protector and provider (Genesis 15:1). And when we tithe, *we enter into covenant with our fellow believers* that we will play our part, no matter how great or how small, to see that the work of the church is financed in the earth. Tithing is a covenant that we make with God and with fellow believers.

In Genesis 14 Abram "lifted up his hand to the Most High God" when he tithed, which is another way of saying that he made an oath before God. When we come before God each Lord's Day, we must come before Him prepared to lift up our hand and present our tithe to Him as an expression of our loyalty to Him and to His people.

Genesis 14 also shows that tithing is directly related to Communion. In Genesis 14, God's priest, Melchizedec, presented Abraham with bread and wine, which was much more than mere refreshments. It was a priestly meal, a peace offering of thanksgiving to the Lord. This meal was a prototype of Communion, the New Covenant meal Jesus instituted at the Last Supper (Matthew 26:26).

When Melchizedec presented the bread and wine to Abraham, he pronounced a blessing upon him: "Blessed be Abram of the Most High God, possessor of heaven and earth." Abraham responded to this blessing by offering his tithe to the Lord. This entire transaction is sacramental and covenantal.

Tithing is connected to Communion, and Communion is about communion. In other words, Communion is about connecting spiritually, and part of that connection is our agreement to tithe in solidarity with other believers. To put it bluntly, there is no free ride. Everyone should be doing their part to finance the work of the church in the earth.

One of the most incredible aspects of tithing is how it creates a channel for blessing to flow from heaven into earth. As Malachi attests, tithing opens up "the windows of heaven" (Malachi 3). Tithing opens up the flow of God's blessing into our lives.

This individual blessing then flows into the corporate body of Christ. When we stand as the church, lifting up our hands to God and presenting our tithe to Him in worship, the blessing of God breaks through into the church and flows throughout the congregation. As it flows, the spirit of poverty is broken. There is so much more to discuss here, but for now we must grasp the salient point that giving is much more than what we do alone in the privacy of our own checkbook. We are connected when we tithe.

Serve. Third, when we tithe, we serve others. When we lift up our hands to tithe, we also lift up the hands of others, the "hands that hang down" (Hebrews 12:12). The tithe helps the needy in many ways.

First of all, our tithe is given to finance the priestly ministry of the church. The primary use of the tithe is the financial maintenance of full-time ministry, which includes the pastor and any elders that may serve the church full-time.

Then, the tithe may also be directed toward "widows indeed," which are those widows over age sixty that are taken on "the list" because they are financially destitute and have no other means of support (I Timothy 5:3-16).

The tithe may also be directed toward helping the poor, though the primary means of helping the poor is almsgiving. In each of these uses, tithing is a wonderful way of connecting with the people of God, of standing together to support those in need.

Offerings

In addition to tithing, the people of God are taught to bring the Lord "freewill offerings" that are above and beyond the regular tithe. In our church, these offerings are allocated to pay for property and buildings, for utilities and regular operating costs. The tithe is reserved for the ministry, for "widows indeed" and for the poor. The tithe was never intended to pay for property and maintain buildings. In the Old Covenant, God commanded His people to bring an additional offering to cover the costs of maintaining the Temple. We follow the same principle.

Our church family is committed to giving a freewill offering above their tithe. Some members give a flat percentage of their income above their tithe—for example, three percent, five percent or so. Others give a flat, set amount. All that we ask is that everyone give a consistent amount on a consistent basis so that our church finances do not fluctuate wildly in an unpredictable manner. We are all connected, and when some do not do their part, we all experience a financial wild ride!

Alms

One aspect of Christian giving that is broadly neglected is almsgiving. Giving alms is simply giving to help the poor. It is fascinating to study Jesus' teaching on money and discover that He talked more about giving to the poor than any other form of giving. God cares deeply about the plight of the needy, and He measures the depth of our love by our compassion upon the poor. Certainly it is possible to give to the poor without love (I Corinthians 13:2), but it is not possible to truly love without giving to the poor.

In fact, it seems clear that almsgiving is an advanced level of giving that most clearly reflects the heart of God to the world, and it is here, in almsgiving, that the full blessing of God begins to flow into our lives. If tithing opens the windows of heaven, almsgiving opens its floodgates! This is a dimension of giving that most Christians never experience because they feel that they have done their part when they tithe and give a nominal offering.

Step out by faith into the realm of giving to the poor, of "setting aside the corners of your field" by reserving a small portion of your weekly paycheck to be set aside for the poor, and you will find that God will become very interested in your finances. He is looking for those who will become channels of His mercy to those who have no one to help them. No matter how small your alms may be at first, give what you can a little at a time and see how God takes notice.

There is much to discuss about financial stewardship, but for now it is enough just to grasp the point that koinonia is lived out through giving. We **CONNECT** when we give.

CHAPTER SEVEN

EDIFYING THE BODY

INTRODUCTION

We have considered how the church connects as the body of Christ and the way this connection is lived out in what the New Testament writers called "koinonia." Now, we should approach the idea of how the Holy Spirit distributes gifts and callings to individual believers to facilitate koinonia so that the church may be edified (built up).

We shall consider two primary passages of scripture, Romans 12 and I Corinthians 12-14, but we shall begin with another brief look at Ephesians 4 where the authority and power of Christ's ascension and exaltation flows out into the church as spiritual gifts. We shall note how that this distribution of spiritual gifts is the means by which the church is built up in the earth and is the catalyst for the reconciliation of heaven and earth, which is the eternal purpose of God (Ephesians 1:10). The church is built and God's purpose is fulfilled through Spirit-gifted people. Believers are the instruments of God's will.

EPHESIANS 4

Take a moment to read Ephesians 4:1-16. Read it carefully and slowly. Ask the Holy Spirit to open up the text to your understanding. There is much here that controls the way we see the role we play advancing the kingdom of God in the earth. This is a passage to which we must return often as we preach and pray the purpose of God.

In this text, Paul the Apostle shows us how eschatological unity (*eschatos* is the Greek word for "last") of the church is effected by the indwelling power of the Spirit. The eschatological unity of the church is the final state of ecclesial unity that the church shall attain prior to the Second Coming. Jesus prayed for ecclesial unity in John 17, and the Holy Spirit was poured out at Pentecost to make it happen. Thus, ecclesial unity *will* be accomplished prior to Christ's return. Ephesians 4 shows us how it happens.

Paul begins by exhorting us to seek Christian unity in our daily lives. He urges us to "walk in a manner worthy of the calling to which you have been called, with all humility and gentleness, with patience, bearing with one another in love, eager to maintain the unity of the Spirit in the bond of peace" (vs. 1-3). The unity of the Spirit flows from the inherent unity that we all possess because we are all baptized by one Spirit into the body of Christ. We are one family because we have one Father.

However, this fundamental unity of the Spirit must be maintained by deliberate effort, and when it is maintained, it grows into the mature unity that Paul calls "the unity of the faith" (v. 13). Grasp this point: the unity of the Spirit grows into the unity of the faith.

The important point of Ephesians 4, though, is *how* this unity of the Spirit becomes the unity of the faith: "But grace was given to each one of us according to the measure of Christ's gift" (v. 7). Paul tells us that Christ ascended into the heavens and graciously poured out His gifts upon believers through the Holy Spirit (v. 8). The specific gifts that Paul lists here are ministry gifts, such as apostles, prophets, evangelists, pastors and teachers. Elsewhere Paul lists many more gifts with a much broader scope of Christian service. However, all gifts are received the same way: Christ Jesus bestows the gifts from His heavenly throne via the indwelling presence of the Holy Spirit.

The ascended and exalted Christ is omnipresenced in the earth through mediation of the Holy Spirit, and His gifts are distributed through the body as the actual, personal ministry of Christ in the earth through believers. When we minister in the gifts of the Spirit, we are allowing Christ Himself to minister through us. Gifts of the Spirit are not about what we do, but they are about what we allow Christ to do through us.

When the gifts of Christ are fully flowing through the church, and individual believers are truly ministering as Christ called them to do, then the body of Christ is "perfected" (made mature) and "edified" (built up) as the universal church fully manifesting the glory of God to all creation.

Paul describes this maturity as "the unity of the faith" and "the knowledge of the Son of God." He calls it "mature manhood" that attains "to the measure of the stature of the fullness of Christ." When the church reaches this stage of maturity, we will "no longer be children, tossed to and fro by the waves and carried about by every wind of doctrine, by human cunning, by craftiness in deceitful schemes." Rather, the church shall be known to speak "the truth in love" and "to grow up in every way into him who is the head, into Christ."

When this happens, then the church will be properly aligned in relationship with Christ, "from whom the whole body, joined and held together by every joint with which it is equipped, when each part is working properly, makes the body grow so that it builds itself up in love." This is the eschatological unity that is predestined to happen within the church through the indwelling power of the Holy Spirit. The church is a "self-edifying" organism that grows itself up in Christ as the Spirit of Christ develops the gifts of its individual members. The church grows as its members grow.

The exploitation of gifts (and we mean *exploitation* in its positive sense) is the means by which the church grows. The gifts are not incidental to the life of the church, given just to improve the quality of ecclesiastical life and smooth the rugged pathway to heaven. No, the gifts of the Spirit *are* the way to heaven, the catalyst of church growth. And church growth is the catalyst of the resurrection and new creation. The perfection of the church is what triggers the fullness of all things that precipitates the end of history. (*That* is another topic for another time!)

We are not overstating the case when we say that the working of the gifts of the Spirit within the church is absolutely essential to the life and ministry of the church. The church *cannot* be edified without it.

In a moment, we shall consider the how the gifts of the Spirit work through individuals, developing their latent potential and maturing their personalities for service in the kingdom. And that is all well and good in its place. But for now, we must nail down the point that spiritual gifts are for the wellbeing and growth of the body, not just for individual growth and self-actualization. Spiritual gifts flow through individuals, but they flow *through* individuals to the church. Spiritual gifts are given *through* individuals *to* the church. The church, and, ultimately, the world to whom the church ministers, is the beneficiary of the gifts.

All spiritual gifts are given to edify the church. Spiritual gifts are not primarily for personal blessing, though each person shares in the blessing as they minister to the church. Spiritual gifts are primarily for the blessing of the people of God, and through the people of God, the blessing of all nations. To put it bluntly, spiritual gifts are not about you and me. Spiritual gifts are about the body of Christ and the new creation.

Jesus sends forth His Spirit from His throne in heaven into the church, and the Spirit infuses the human spirit of individual believers with divine power that awakens latent human potential that is distorted and degraded by sin and death. When this individual potential is awakened and developed by the Spirit, each believer contributes his or her own unique spiritual contribution to the life of the church, and all believers benefit from each contribution.

By this process of mutual giftedness, which is another aspect of koinonia, the church is strengthened and edified. This process occurs in three stages: (1) Jesus sends forth His gifts by the Spirit into individual believers; (2) the Spirit awakens latent potential within their human spirit; and (3) the spiritual gifts are shared with the body of Christ and the church is built up as the body of Christ to serve the world in its redemptive task. If we consider this process for a moment, we can readily see how spiritual giftedness is absolutely essential to the redemptive work of Christ and the church.

Now, let's take a moment to look at two well-known passages that deal with spiritual gifts, Romans 12 and I Corinthians 12-14.

ROMANS 12

As we shall see, I Corinthians 12 deals with gifts of the Spirit that are used primarily in the public worship service. Romans 12, on the other hand, deals with gifts of the Spirit in a more general sense, with gifts that are used both in public worship and outside settings. Look at the text:

> For by the grace given to me I say to everyone among you not to think of himself more highly than he ought to think, but to think with sober judgment, each according to the measure of faith that God has assigned. For as in one body we have many members, and the members do not all have the same function, so we, though many, are one body in Christ, and individually members one of another. Having gifts that differ according to the grace given to us, let us use them: if prophecy, in proportion to our faith; if service, in our serving; the one who teaches, in his teaching; the one who exhorts, in his exhortation; the one who contributes, in generosity; the one who leads, with zeal; the one who does acts of mercy, with cheerfulness. (Romans 12:3-8)

Our gifts "differ according to the grace given to us." Paul lists prophecy, service, teaching, exhortation, contributions, leading, and acts of mercy. Many of these things are ordinary enough, occurring in everyday life. But for Paul, they become extraordinary when given by the grace of the Spirit and empowered by the faith of Jesus Christ to edify the body of Christ and minister to the world. The ordinary good deeds of the average man become a "living sacrifice" (v. 2) when they are empowered by the Spirit in the service of Christ to the glory of God.

This is important. Many Christians never see the extraordinary potential that lies latent within them because they are presently unable to evaluate their abilities honestly. They must learn to think of themselves as they "ought to think" with "sober judgment, each according to the measure of faith that God has assigned." No doubt, we must not think of ourselves "more highly than we ought to think"—in other words, we should not see our gifts as being for our own self-aggrandizement and not for the good of the body. But on the other hand, neither should we think of ourselves as *less* than we ought to think. We should not regard the spiritual gifts we have received as nothing more than ordinary abilities that we can use or neglect at will. The gifts we have received have been given so that we may serve the body of Christ for the good of the world.

I CORINTHIANS 12-14

In I Corinthians 12-14, Paul addresses the operation of the gifts of the Spirit within the public worship service. Read I Corinthians chapters 12-14 very carefully. Do not skim over these passages. Read them several times over while praying for understanding. It is important to capture the essence of Paul's teaching, particularly chapter 13 where he shows us that love must be the true motive of spiritual gifts.

We do not have the space here to offer a detailed discussion of these chapters. For now, let's look at the list of gifts that Paul describes as operating in the public worship service. This will at least help us see the principal idea of our present study: spiritual gifts help the church *connect* as the body of Christ.

Paul lists several gifts (each gift is emboldened in the text for emphasis):

> Now there are varieties of gifts, but the same Spirit; and there are varieties of service, but the same Lord; and there are varieties of activities, but it is the same God who empowers them all in everyone. To each is given the manifestation of the Spirit for the common good. For to one is given through the Spirit **the utterance of wisdom**, and to another **the utterance of knowledge** according to the same Spirit, to another **faith** by the same Spirit, to another **gifts of healing** by the one Spirit, to another **the working of miracles**, to another **prophecy**, to another **the ability to distinguish between spirits**, to another **various kinds of tongues**, to another **the interpretation of tongues**. All these are empowered by one and the same Spirit, who apportions to each one individually as he wills. (I Corinthians 12:4-11)

There are "varieties" of gifts, service and activities, but it is the one God-Lord-Spirit who "empowers them all in everyone." And all of these gifts are manifestations of the Spirit that are given "for the common good." God "apportions to each one individually as He wills."

All of this underscores the fact that there is a powerful unity-in-diversity that operates in the church when the gifts of the Spirit are working through many different members within one, unified body. It is much like an orchestra: each instrument within the orchestra plays the same music in very different ways. And when each instrument plays the music in its own unique way, the blend of diversity creates breathtaking beauty. This does not mean, of course, that each instrument, by thinking too highly of itself, may play its own tune. No, that would be chaos. The instruments must be joined together in the unified purpose of playing the same music while expressing it in unique and diverse ways. That is real music.

CONCLUSION

There are many different passages that describe gifts of the Spirit. We do not have space here to discuss any of them further. However, the point of this lesson is not to provide an exhaustive study on spiritual gifts. There are volumes of resources available on the topic. No, our point here is to show that covenant membership in Cornerstone Apostolic Church entails a commitment on our part to "connect" with the congregation by bringing our own personal gifts and abilities to the table.

Spiritual maturity comes when believers realize that they were not called to the church just so the church could minister to them, though certainly it *does* minister to them. But true breakthrough in spiritual growth comes when the believer realizes that they are called to be a giver, not just a taker; a contributor, not just a recipient. It is more blessed to give than to receive.

God did not place us in this church just to save us from our sins and from hell. He certainly saves us from both. But

He did not *save* us just to *save* us. He saved us to *use* us. He has placed within every believer certain key gifts and abilities that the church desperately needs in order to become the full-grown body of Christ. Jesus within you is developing a degree of glory that can only be fully realized *in you*. Each of us possesses a unique prism of personality that refracts the light of God's glory in a beautifully special way. The church cannot be the church in its fullness without the individual contribution of its members.

What do you bring to the table? If you are at the table, you bring *something*. What is it? Think about it. Pray about it. And most of all, develop a "contributor attitude" that insists on seeing the church as a place to become all God wants you to be so that you can play your part in fulfilling the mission of this local church. Insist on "connecting" with the church by contributing to the church through the gifts of the Spirit.

CHAPTER EIGHT

THE COMMUNION OF THE SAINTS

INTRODUCTION

Earlier, we spoke about "communion" in the "ordinary" and the "proper" sense. Ordinary communion is the fellowship (koinonia) we share as believers. Proper Communion is the Lord's Supper. In this section we shall speak of communion in one more sense. We shall consider the idea of communion as the universal and eschatological connectedness of the body of Christ throughout time and space. This may sound a bit exotic at first, but read closely and think through the concepts presented, and I think you will be thrilled at the implications. The church of Jesus Christ is much more glorious than we can even imagine!

CONNECTED UNIVERSALLY

The church is connected in heaven and in earth. And we mean by this that the church is connected in real fellowship with the saints that are in heaven awaiting the resurrection and with all the saints that worship in every nation in the earth. When we gather to worship every Lord's Day, we are gathered together with the saints in heaven and the saints in every nation. This gathering is accomplished by the unity of the Spirit. Though we may not even be aware of it, the one Spirit that dwells in us in our local congregation is the same Spirit that dwells in every believer in heaven and earth and makes us one in spiritual union.

Universal unity has both a vertical and a horizontal aspect. We are one with the saints in heaven (vertical unity), and we are one with the saints presently living on the earth (horizontal unity). Let's look at the easy part first, the horizontal unity that we have on earth.

Horizontal Unity

It is fairly straightforward to assert that we are joined together by the Spirit with all believers presently living upon the earth. Most of us can grasp that easy enough. Though I may not see my brothers and sisters in China, for example, I can still see how the one Spirit of God makes us one as we worship.

What I may not see so easily, though, is that our unity is more than merely worshipping at the same time. In fact, most worship that happens in the earth throughout the Lord's Day is not happening at the same time. The morning sun awakens the dawn each Sunday with praises that begin in the lands farthest east, and as the sun makes its journey through the circuit of the earth, there is an unbroken chorus of worship that fills every hour of the day. Worship happens all day, but it happens at different times throughout the day. So, our oneness in worship is not just the oneness of a spiritual "simulcast."

No, there is something bigger happening when we worship as one body. The unity of the Spirit—the *Holy Spirit*—creates an ontological unity of spirits, the spirits of believers. Believers are spiritually joined together, and their human spirits flow into one another in an actual, metaphysical communion that makes the body of Christ one.

Though no one loses their individuality, yet their individuality is augmented as gifts and influences from within a local congregation and around the world flow throughout the body of Christ. This is what Paul means when he tells us that we are one body, joined together by one spirit. He teaches us that the actions of one believer can affect the spirit of every other believer and the spirit of the entire church.

Consider his warning in I Corinthians 6:

> Do you not know that your bodies are members of Christ? Shall I then take the members of Christ and make them members of a prostitute? Never! Or do you not know that he who is joined to a prostitute becomes one body with her? For, as it is written, "The two will become one flesh." But he who is joined to the Lord becomes one spirit with him. (I Corinthians 6:15-17)

How are the members of Christ made the members of a prostitute? By the communion of human spirits. Our spirits are united together even when we do not realize it.

Paul also speaks of being united spiritually with his churches even though he was not physically present:

> For though absent in body, I am present in spirit; and as if present, I have already pronounced judgment on the one who did such a thing. When you are assembled in the name of the Lord Jesus and my spirit is present, with the

power of our Lord Jesus, you are to deliver this man to Satan for the destruction of the flesh, so that his spirit may be saved in the day of the Lord. (I Corinthians 5:3-5)

For though I am absent in body, yet I am with you in spirit, rejoicing to see your good order and the firmness of your faith in Christ. (Colossians 2:5)

There is more here than just Paul thinking fond thoughts about the church in his mind. No, Paul considered that he was actually present in some sense when they gathered together: "My spirit is present."

We see other examples of this in Scripture. Elisha told his servant, Gehazi, that his spirit went out with him when he pursued Naaman the Leper to satisfy his greed. Elisha asked Elijah to allow him to receive a double portion of Elijah's spirit. Jesus declared that the spirit of Elijah was upon John the Baptist. God told Moses that He would take the spirit of Moses and put it upon the elders of Israel. In each of these cases, there is spiritual connectivity between people. The human spirit of man *influences* the spirit of others. It flows into them and affects their personal existence.

In our rationalistic, Western mindset we tend to diminish, if not dismiss altogether, the spiritual connectivity of human beings. We speak of things like "morale," "school spirit" and "feeling vibes" from someone, even "sensing their aura," but we rarely fully comprehend the implications of what we are saying: our human spirits are connected.

One writer compared this to fish in the sea. Fish live in a world that is fluid and filled with motion. But fish are probably not even aware of the water around them that connects them to every other fish. The water is their atmosphere. One fish flicks his tail and another fish across the pond wobbles in the water. Does the fish know what moved him? Probably not. But he moved, nonetheless. We are the same. We are affected by spiritual realities that we live in every day but about which we understand very little.

Moreover, when we receive the Holy Spirit, this invisible connection is powerfully intensified. We are made one by the Spirit. We become "one spirit" with the Lord, and when we are made one with Him, we are made one with everyone that is one with Him. This is more than an abstract, metaphorical oneness, mere unity of mind and purpose. No, this is an actual, ontological oneness of spirit that joins us together as the body of Christ.

When we receive the Holy Spirit, we receive the glorified human spirit of Jesus Christ. When Jesus ascended into heaven, His human spirit was fully glorified by the indwelling Spirit of God the Father, and His human spirit was sent by God into the hearts of believers at Pentecost: "And because you are sons, God has sent the Spirit of his Son into our hearts, crying, 'Abba! Father!'" (Galatians 4:6). God the Father flows out of Himself as projected image, which is Jesus Christ. Thus, the human spirit of Jesus is the incarnational expression of God's eternal Spirit.

Jesus is God the Father manifest as human being (spirit-soul-body). Then, the human spirit of Jesus, filled with the fullness of the Spirit of God, flows out into the church as the Holy Spirit. Jesus "proceeds and comes forth from the Father," and the Holy Spirit proceeds from both the Father and the Son. So, when we receive the Holy Spirit, we are receiving the Spirit of God and the Spirit of Christ, which, of course, are one Spirit flowing out from God through Christ as the Holy Spirit.

However, there is more. When we receive the Spirit of Christ, we receive the Spirit of the body of Christ. The Spirit of the body of Christ is the communion of the Spirit of Christ flowing through the human spirit of every individual believer forming them into one covenantal, existential body.

So, when we are "baptized by one Spirit into one body," we are baptized into communion with every other believer through whom the Holy Spirit is flowing. We are made one with one another just as God and Christ are made one (John 17), and this oneness causes the life of the body to flow throughout the body so that the body edifies itself in love (Ephesians 4; Colossians 2). As we discussed above, the giftedness of the body flows through the body, and we contribute to one another's spiritual strength and wellbeing. We *influence* (flow into) one another.

This *influence* occurs every time we gather together with other believers. But here is the amazing thing: this influence knows no boundaries. It is universal. Unity happens throughout the earth. Certainly, the unity of the church is stronger where people are gathered together in proximate location, but we cannot overlook the fact that the Spirit is flowing throughout the church in every nation. Cornerstone Apostolic Church is united by the Spirit with every other congregation that preaches the gospel of Christ in this city and in every nation.

Vertical Unity

The second aspect of universal connectedness is the fact that we are connected with the saints in heaven that are in presence of Christ awaiting the resurrection. Those that die in Christ go to be with Him in heaven until the resurrection when they shall awaken in a moment and rise to meet Him in the air (I Thessalonians 4). Paul told the church that the intermediate state was "to be absent from the body" and "present with Christ" (II Corinthians 5:6-8). It is interesting that Paul uses the same language of "absent" and "present" to describe his spiritual involvement in the church at Corinth, which we read about above (I Corinthians 5:3-5).

There is a lot of discussion about the intermediate state, the state of those that are dead in Christ awaiting the resurrection. Of course, we do not have space here to do a full study of the subject. But we can at least acknowledge that those who await the resurrection are in the presence of Christ and are consciously aware of those on earth. Consider three things:

1. Paul speaks of being present with Christ and absent from the body in the same terms that he speaks to the church at Corinth about his ongoing involvement in their affairs. This tells me that being absent in the body does not mean that a person is fully cut off from spiritual involvement. Thus, it is biblically possible to see that Paul could now be absent in the body and present with Christ awaiting the resurrection while still involved in the spirit with the church in the earth.

2. John sees the righteous "under the altar" in heaven crying out for vengeance upon God's enemies (Revelation 6:9). These are the righteous dead, and they are most certainly conscious and aware of events

upon the earth. Also, John speaks with a man that he mistakes for an angel. The man calls himself a "fellow servant" (Revelation 19:10). This man was "dead" and in the presence of Christ, and yet he was actively engaged in the work of God upon the earth.

3. Hebrews 12 speaks of those that gather together with the church when we worship:

> But you have come to Mount Zion and to the city of the living God, the heavenly Jerusalem, and to innumerable angels in festal gathering, and to the assembly of the firstborn who are enrolled in heaven, and to God, the judge of all, and to the spirits of the righteous made perfect, and to Jesus, the mediator of a new covenant, and to the sprinkled blood that speaks a better word than the blood of Abel. (Hebrews 12:22-24)

> When we worship, we are gathered with "innumerable angels," "the assembly of the firstborn who are enrolled in heaven," and with "the spirits of the righteous made perfect." The assembly of the firstborn could reasonable be interpreted as those still on earth, but the "spirits of the righteous made perfect" can only be speaking of the dead in Christ, the "great cloud of witnesses" described in Hebrews 12:1-3, those listed in "the Hall of Faith" in Hebrews 11.

What does this mean? It means that there is vertical unity within the church. We are not only connected by the Spirit to those who call on the name of the Lord throughout the earth, but we are connected to the saints in heaven, including the

Old Testament saints that were the "captivity led captive" when Jesus ascended (Ephesians 4).

When we gather to worship, we are surrounded by an innumerable company of angels and by the spirits of "just men made perfect," as the King James Version puts it. We are worshipping with the saints of old from Abel to Moses to Peter and Paul. Indeed, we are worshipping with those that have died in Christ within recent memory. The faithful members of this congregation that have gone to be with the Lord in the last few years are still gathering with us every Sunday. They are still actively involved in the work of God in Fort Worth, praying, interceding and rejoicing with us as we celebrate the goodness of God.

Furthermore—and this is where it gets goosebumpy!—we share in one spirit with the saints of God in heaven. The same Holy Spirit that communicates edification horizontally throughout the body of Christ on the earth mediates the Spirit of the church from the saints in heaven to the saints upon the earth. This may seem astounding, but I think the same spirit that was within Peter and Paul still flows throughout the church today.

Of course, we must be careful to avoid the excesses of many professing Christians who have been deceived into thinking that they should pray to the saints or expect that the saints are personally with them as protective guardians and counselors. This goes too far. But just because some have gone too far does not mean for a moment that we should surrender the truth that the biblical evidence suggests: we are gathered together in one body by one Spirit with the saints in all of heaven and all of earth. *That* is astounding!

We should consider this a bit farther in the next section on how the church is connected *eschatologically*.

CONNECTED ESCHATOLOGICALLY

First, let's have a fuller definition of "Eschatology." That might help! "Eschatology" is just a fancy word for "the study of last things" from the Greek words *eschatos* and *logos*. So, when we talk about the "eschatological unity" of the church, we are talking about the unity that the present church has with the future when God makes all things new in the resurrection. If universal unity has to do with unity in *space* (heaven and earth), then eschatological unity has to do with unity in *time*.

The church at present stands in solidarity with the resurrected church of the future. And this is more than just a matter of God viewing the present church in terms of what it shall be, though that is certainly true. No, this present-future continuity has to do with the fact that what is coming is here already in the firstfruits of the Spirit. Just as we can say that the apple tree exists within the apple seed, so the future church exists within the present church.

Moreover, the future is a heavenly future when heaven shall come to earth and all things shall be made new. This means that the future for earth already exists *now* in heaven. It simply must be realized in the earth.

And this leads to another point: the future that is coming is a predestined future that has always existed in God's eternal purpose. This means that the future flows out of the past. Destiny and history merge in the eternal purpose of God. Now, that is heavy stuff, no doubt, but it is exactly what Paul touched on in Ephesians 1-3. If you are interested in this idea, read and pray your way through Ephesians again and again until it begins to come into focus.

So, the eschatological church not only stands in perfect continuity with the future, but it also stands in perfect continuity with the past. This means that the present church cannot escape the past or the future, where we have been and where we are going. The past is pushing us, and the future is pulling us, and we stand in the middle suspended in the present. But we are not really suspended as if we have no role to play, for we build upon the past and erect our future.

We must have healthy respect for our history and keen sense of our destiny. We are in fellowship with our fathers in the faith not only because they are in the bleachers watching us run on the field below, but because their record on the field determines where we are in the game. We inherit our fathers' score. However, we are also in fellowship with future generations because they will inherit our score. The progress that has been made in the past controls present momentum. The same is true for us: we are affecting our children for good or evil depending on how we run the race.

Above, we talked about how the church exists in a universal spiritual communion where saints in heaven and earth share in one Spirit that flows through individual believers. This means that Joe and Bill may worship across the building from one another—or, even across the world from one another—but one Spirit unites both men. Bill's spirit is in communion with Joe's spirit, and each is affected by the other.

The Spirit gives certain gifts to Joe, and he ministers to Bill. Not only does Bill receive the particular ministry that Joe shared, but Bill, if he will yield himself to the communion of the saints, will receive *Joe's spirit* into his own, and Joe's giftedness will augment Bill's spirit. Just like two musicians collaborate and augment one another's abilities and bring out latent creativity, so two Christians "provoke one another" and increase one another in love. Of course, this requires fellowship, but even two men who have never met may build one another through prayer. It happens all the time!

This sort of spiritual communion also occurs in an eschatological sense. The present church stands in continuity with the past, and "the spirits of just men made perfect" come to rest upon men and women in the present. We looked at several scriptures earlier where the spirits of godly men rested upon other men. The spirit of Moses, Elijah, Elisha, Paul, etc. rested upon their heirs. It seems to me that this is still true today.

Again, we must be careful not to take this to an extreme, but there are many instances where the spirits of righteous people from the past seemed to rest upon men and women as they ministered in power that transcended their time. It seems sometimes that the mantle of the fathers may come to rest upon the sons.

It is also true that this generation is laying up spiritual treasures that will be available to future generations. We are building memorials of prayer and fasting, of teaching and fellowship that will be the legacy we pass to the next generation. And as the Lord tarries, we will go on to be with the Lord, and the next generation will carry our baton attempting to perfect our score. What sort of legacy are we leaving behind?

One final thing on eschatological unity: when we speak of the eschatological unity of the church, we must at least mention again the prophesied unity of Ephesians 4. Paul describes the church in its eschatological state, the church of the last days, the church for which Christ will return, as a church that is fully mature and perfectly manifesting the image of God in Christ.

This perfect church is the future church, and it is the pattern by which the present church should be measured. The church does not seek to imitate the world, to mold itself after the pattern of business, politics, the academy or the theatre. The church should be looking at Christ in the heavens as the perfect pattern of what the church should be. In Revelation, John saw the church "coming down from God out of heaven." That is the church that awaits us in the future, and that future is already at work within us now.

We would be untrue to our own nature to seek to become anything else. Can the apple sapling look to the mighty oak and wistfully seek to be shaped in its pattern? Not a chance! The apple bears in its seed the ultimate shape of its destiny. The same is true of the church. Let us hold fast to our origins and our destiny. We have a past and a future that are both centered in Christ. Let us not forsake Him.

CONCLUSION

The church is connected as both the eschatological and universal church. The church stands together in continuity with the past and the future, and it stands in solidarity with all believers in every nation. God has placed us strategically in our place both chronologically and geographically so that we may play our individual part in the overall ministry and mission of the church. We share in the communion of the saints from eternity past in the purpose of God, to Abel as the first earthly believer, all the way to the Second Coming when the entire church shall be "churched" together with the Lord forever. We are connected with believers in the past, present and future.

It is important to grasp the "communicable nature" of the human spirit, especially when empowered by the Holy Spirit. When we receive the Holy Spirit, we receive the human spirit of Christ glorified and filled with the fullness of God. But we also "tap in" to the collective spirit of the church, which is the composite spiritual existence of all believers throughout past and future history and presently worshipping in the earth filled with the Spirit. Thus, we are connected in a way much greater than we even see. We must understand the spiritual interconnectivity of the body of Christ. When we receive the Holy Spirit, we receive the spirit of the entire church. When we connect, we receive the giftedness of the people with whom we are connected. This giftedness flows through the body both vertically and horizontally. It is a cruciform unity.

Part Three: Serve

CHAPTER NINE

CHRISTIAN SERVICE AND THE KINGDOM OF GOD

INTRODUCTION

At Cornerstone Apostolic Church, we believe that a deep relationship with God will affect our relationship with fellow Christians. In other words, we believe that those who **WORSHIP** together will **CONNECT** together. However, the development of relationships does not end when we walk out the doors of the sanctuary. Our love for God and for one another goes with us when we leave Sunday service, and our love for God and one another flows out into the world as love for the world. We believe that the work of the church is fully complete when it flows out as **WORSHIP** → **CONNECT** → **SERVE**.

The last four lessons in this series will address the need for every Christian to move along in the continuum from worshipping God to connecting with fellow believers to serving in the world. We shall consider Christian service in three primary areas: (1) serving the family; (2) serving the church; and (3) serving the world. First, however, let's consider the biblical basis for Christian service and how serving brings the kingdom of God to earth.

SALT AND LIGHT

The church must be more than merely *different* in the world. The church must make a *difference* in the world. Jesus said that the church is like "salt" and "light." He used these metaphors to illustrate the difference believers should make in the lives of people around them. Salt and light affect everything they touch. The church must do the same. Look carefully at Jesus' words:

> You are the salt of the earth, but if salt has lost its taste, how shall its saltiness be restored? It is no longer good for anything except to be thrown out and trampled under people's feet. You are the light of the world. A city set on a hill cannot be hidden. Nor do people light a lamp and put it under a basket, but on a stand, and it gives light to all in the house. In the same way, let your light shine before others, so that they may see your good works and give glory to your Father who is in heaven. (Matthew 5:13–16)

"Let your shine before others." It has always been the will of God that His people should make a difference. From the beginning, God has always placed His people in strategic locations throughout the world and in society so that they might draw the eyes of men and women to the glory of God. Think of Joseph in the court of Pharaoh, or Daniel ruling as Prime Minister of Babylon and Persia. Think of Solomon astounding the Queen of Sheba with the glory of his kingdom and his manner of worship. Think of Elisha ministering to pagan kings and generals. There are numerous biblical examples of God's people making a difference in the world.

God told Israel that He would cause all nations to behold His glory in their faithful obedience to His law. Moreover, all of Israel's prophets understood clearly that God's purpose with Israel had always been that pagan nations would come to worship the one true God through Israel's ministry in the world.

For example, God was insistent that Israel should show benevolence to the foreigners in her midst. The "law of the stranger" was explicit: Israel must do good to those from other nations that sojourned within her borders. God called His people to serve the world in order to draw all nations to Him.

Salt and light influence everything they touch. The church must do the same. We are salt and light in the world by serving the world at the point of its need. We cannot influence the world by merely gathering to worship and connect with one another. We must go into the world and actually make a difference. We do this by serving.

FAITH WITHOUT WORKS IS DEAD

The apostle James taught that true faith—that is, Christian faith—is a faith that is manifest in works. And the works in which faith is manifest are very practical works, things like feeding the hungry and clothing the naked. Look at the text:

> What good is it, my brothers, if someone says he has faith but does not have works? Can that faith save him? If

a brother or sister is poorly clothed and lacking in daily food, and one of you says to them, "Go in peace, be warmed and filled," without giving them the things needed for the body, what good is that? So also faith by itself, if it does not have works, is dead. But someone will say, "You have faith and I have works." Show me your faith apart from your works, and I will show you my faith by my works. You believe that God is one; you do well. Even the demons believe—and shudder! Do you want to be shown, you foolish person, that faith apart from works is useless? Was not Abraham our father justified by works when he offered up his son Isaac on the altar? You see that faith was active along with his works, and faith was completed by his works; and the Scripture was fulfilled that says, "Abraham believed God, and it was counted to him as righteousness"—and he was called a friend of God. You see that a person is justified by works and not by faith alone. And in the same way was not also Rahab the prostitute justified by works when she received the messengers and sent them out by another way? For as the body apart from the spirit is dead, so also faith apart from works. (James 2:14–26)

James says that our faith is not "complete" if our faith is not lived out ministering to people in need. Our faith is made perfect in Christian service.

Many Christians see Christianity as a private faith that never goes much beyond a personal relationship with Jesus Christ. For many believers, just escaping this wicked world and "going to heaven when they die" is salvation enough. But Jesus calls us to a much greater salvation, a much more radical faith, a faith that takes seriously Christian ministry in the world, a faith that engages the culture and influences society. This sort of faith is a robust faith that goes far beyond an anemic Christianity that is powerless to make a difference prior to the Second Coming. This sort of faith is faith in action, faith that serves.

We are saved by faith. And the salvation that our faith brings is "full gospel" salvation, a salvation—or, deliverance—that declares the good news of Jesus' resurrection in every realm of life.

Think of it like this: when Jesus comes again, all things will be made new. Every realm of life, every function of culture and society, will be transformed in the glorification of all creation (Romans 8). This will occur when Jesus returns to rule forever upon the earth. But that future reality has already broken in upon present history through the in-time, in-space resurrection of Jesus two thousand years ago. When the Holy Spirit was poured out at Pentecost, He brought the power of Christ's resurrection into the hearts of believers, and the future reality of new creation became the present possession of believers in a firstfruit, "earnest of our inheritance" sense. This means that what is coming has already come, and we must expect to live out presently a foretaste experience of the eternal future (Hebrews 6:5).

Consider this: we understand that the fullness of personal sanctification awaits the glorification of our bodies in the future resurrection. In other words, we believe that we will never sin again in the new creation. Yet, we emphatically do not believe that we should wait until Jesus comes again before we start seeing a change in our personal habits and individual manner of life. We may not be perfect yet, but we should be working on it. The same is true of the world. We should not wait until the resurrection before we start expecting to see a change in the world.

The fullness of "cosmic sanctification" may await the resurrection, but the "earnest" of that sanctification has begun already. Think about how much the world has changed in the last two thousand years since the resurrection of Jesus and the spread of Christianity throughout the nations. Caesar wouldn't recognize the world! This is the "salt and light" effect of the Christian faith that is demonstrated by works.

Thus, our salvation by faith must be a holistic salvation that brings the renewal promise of new creation to every realm of life. The gospel we preach declares the good news of Christ's resurrection to "all the world." The gospel—the same gospel preached to Abraham that all nations would be blessed through his children (Galatians 3:8)—is preached to the poor, the sick, the addicted, the abused, the oppressed, the demon possessed, and all who are imprisoned in the grip of sin and death. The day of salvation has come, and all nations shall be blessed in Christ. "The Spirit of the Lord God is upon us" to preach salvation to them all (Luke 4).

PREACH THE GOSPEL TO ALL THE WORLD

Jesus commanded us to preach the gospel to the entire world. Look at Mark's account of the Great Commission:

> Afterward he appeared to the eleven themselves as they were reclining at table, and he rebuked them for their unbelief and hardness of heart, because they had not believed those who saw him after he had risen. And he said to them, "Go into all the world and proclaim the gospel to the whole creation. Whoever believes and is

baptized will be saved, but whoever does not believe will be condemned. And these signs will accompany those who believe: in my name they will cast out demons; they will speak in new tongues; they will pick up serpents with their hands; and if they drink any deadly poison, it will not hurt them; they will lay their hands on the sick, and they will recover. So then the Lord Jesus, after he had spoken to them, was taken up into heaven and sat down at the right hand of God. And they went out and preached everywhere, while the Lord worked with them and confirmed the message by accompanying signs. (Mark 16:14-20)

The disciples, and this includes present day believers, were commanded to "go into all the world and proclaim the gospel to the whole creation." This means exactly what it says. We are called to preach the good news of Christ's resurrection to the entire "cosmos." Our gospel is a "cosmic gospel." There is no realm of life excluded from Christ's resurrected rule. This means that the power of the resurrection within us should be affecting every realm of life that we enter as Christians. Our work, our family and our community should be feeling the affects of "salt and light."

We should see every realm of life as subject to Christ. And that includes *everything*: education, vocation, science, medicine, the arts, entertainment, film, literature, technology, architecture, mineral development and natural resource exploration, the environment, space exploration, ecology, geography, culinary arts, mathematics, engineering—you name it! Christ rules over it all, and the church should be preaching gospel salvation to it all. Practice all of these things as Christians—that *is* the gospel.

However, we do not believe that these things can be "saved" in any humanistic way apart from the resurrection of Christ. We do not believe that we can redeem any part of the cosmos without the power of the Cross. As we shall see, this is what the temptation of Jesus was all about in the wilderness. We cannot bring salvation to the world apart from the Cross.

THE KINGDOM OF GOD

When Jesus came in the incarnation, He came feeding the hungry, clothing the naked, healing the sick and casting out devils. No doubt, He rebuked the people for wanting *only* these material blessings, but He never rejected meeting material needs as an invalid form of Christian ministry. Jesus simply insisted that meeting the material needs of man was secondary to meeting his spiritual needs.

There are two extremes here: (1) ignoring spiritual needs and obsessing with only material needs; and (2) ignoring material needs and focusing only on the spiritual. Both extremes are wrong. We must hold both together in perfect balance while understanding that spiritual transformation is primary.

In fact, the temptation in the wilderness was all about how needs were to be met and what sort of ministry to the needy that Jesus' kingdom would have. Look closer at the tests that Jesus faced.

- **Economic power:** The first temptation was about turning stones to bread. This was a temptation to seek power as Messiah through economic means. This temptation addresses the realm of the family, the household (the word "economy" comes from the Greek word "*oikonomos*," which means "law of the house"), for the household has as its primary responsibility putting bread on the table.

- **Religious power:** The second temptation concerned religion and the attempt to become Messiah to Israel by liberating their temple from the control of the corrupt regime of the Rome-collaborating Sadducees. This temptation addresses the realm of the church.

- **Political power:** The third temptation involved the attempt of Satan to persuade Jesus to become Messiah by acquiring political and societal control over the world, the kingdoms of the earth. This temptation addresses the realm of the state.

Jesus rejected Satan's attempt to persuade Him to seek economic, religious and political power as the means of establishing His kingdom in the three governmental realms of the earth: *family*, *church* and *state*. If Jesus had fed the people by turning stones to bread, leapt from the parapet of the temple to lead a religious cleansing, and if He had bowed down to worship Satan so that He could gain immediate political control of the nations, then Jesus could have ruled the world in just a matter of days.

But Christ understood very well that it is the kingdom of the heart that must be conquered first before the kingdoms of the world can be brought under the kingdom of heaven. The grip of sin that enslaves the kingdoms of the world is the cultural and societal outworking of the sins of the human heart. Poverty, idolatry and injustice are all macro-sins that begin with the micro-sins of personal rebellion against the law of God. Thus, Jesus came to convert the hearts of men, and by conversion, change the world one heart at a time.

However—and we must be perfectly clear on this point—Jesus did not reject the idea of feeding the hungry, reforming worship and taking dominion over the kingdoms of the world as a matter of indifference to Christians. In fact, these are the things that He specifically came to do. He just came to do them in a different way than Israel expected Him to. Jesus came to rule over the family, the church and the state, but He came to do so by walking along the pathway of the Cross.

TAKE UP YOUR CROSS

Christian service must be *Christian*. In other words, it must be done as Christ would do it. This means that our Christian service must be more than mere charity or ordinary benevolence. When we feed the hungry, clothe the naked and house the homeless, it must be done in a "whole gospel" manner. We must serve the needy in order to lead them to Christ.

Now, this does *not* mean that we refuse to help people unless they attend our church or believe the gospel. No, we help all who are in need "no-strings-attached." But still, we do so understanding that filling an empty belly is ultimately useless if the hungry are not fed with the bread of life. Our goal is to save the world through the resurrection of Jesus, which can only be personally experienced through repentance, baptism and Holy Spirit infilling.

In order for Christian service to be truly Christian it must *cruciform*. This means that our service to the world must be a "crucified" service that conforms to the shape of the Cross. Jesus commanded those who would be His disciples to deny themselves, take up their cross and follow Him. (Matthew 16:24)

We hear a lot about bearing our cross, but we often miss the most important point of the passage: bearing the cross with Jesus is a matter of carrying the cross for *others,* not for *yourself.* Think about it: Jesus did not carry the cross for His own sins; He carried it for ours. Thus, if we wish to be His disciples, we must be willing to carry the cross for others, not just for self.

This is the heart of Christian service. We carry the cross of Christ for others by loving them as He loved us. Has Jesus loved us enough to meet our needs? Has He fed us? Has He healed us? Has He saved us? Yes, and we must do the same for others. This is true Christian service.

CONCLUSION

The point we must establish starting out in our discussion is that we believe that Christian service is necessary, but that it also necessarily must be done through the power of the Holy Spirit and not merely as humanistic good works. This is very important.

Many believers have avoided Christian service to the world because of a studied and legitimate aversion to Christian "social action" that has been pursued in the past as a utopian scheme for saving the world apart from the power of the gospel. Many Christians have reacted to utopianism with a cloistered pietism that sings "This World Is Not My Home" while expecting that real change will only occur in the world when Jesus comes again. These folks have come to believe that social action is polishing the brass on a sinking ship, and we may as well just save as many sinners as we can, for we are "Getting Ready to Leave This World" as soon as possible.

However, this sort of pietistic quest for personal holiness at the expense of doing anything practical in the world beyond personal evangelism ends up marching along the path of the priest and the Levite in the story of the Good Samaritan. Is it possible that our quest for an escapist holiness ethic can cause us to shut out the cry of those that have fallen among thieves? Possibly. We must reconsider our commitment as Christians to the ministry of Christ in the world. We must reject both utopian social action and pietistic withdrawal from the world and its pain. We must embrace a Christian service that is both *Christian* and *service.*

CHAPTER TEN

SERVING THE FAMILY

INTRODUCTION

The basic premise of our study on **SERVE** is that the church is called to actualize the kingdom of God, the dominion of Christ, in the earth through active, faithful Christian service. Paul teaches us in I Corinthians 15 that Jesus must reign from heaven through the mediation of the Holy Spirit within the church until He has subdued under the body of Christ all of the enemies that God subdued under Christ in the His resurrection—that is to say, *all* of them (cf. Hebrews 2:8, 9). This means that the church shall make an incredible difference in the world prior to the Second Coming.

The kingdom of God is like "leaven in the meal" that starts out small but eventually affects the whole (Matthew 13). Christian service is the way this influence is realized in a practical way in the world. Christian service seeks to meet the needs of people and thereby bring them to faith and repentance. This is the heart and soul of Christian service, as we saw above.

However, Christian service is more than just doing good deeds to strangers. Christian service begins at home. One of the most neglected areas of Christian service is the family. And we mean by this that many Christians excel at serving the world but overlook their own loved ones. At Cornerstone Church, serving the family is the one of the fundamental aspects of our ministry and mission. Indeed, as we shall see, we believe that the kingdom of God cannot come in the earth apart from the generational momentum that is established and increased from within the Christian home.

Cornerstone Apostolic Church is a "family-centered church." This means that we see our church as a "family of families" and that we seek to orient congregational life around the home. Now, this does not mean that our church values only the traditional "nuclear family" of dad, mom and kids. No, we treasure families in whatever form they come, as long as the relationship is not formed in sin.

In fact, we often speak of families as "households" to convey the fact that all families are valued whatever their makeup. The church is made up of single moms and dads, grandparents rearing a grandchild or two, siblings living together, and various family members sharing household space. Everyone should know that their family is a part of the church family, and that every household is a means of advancing the kingdom of God in the earth. This is important to emphasize so that Satan cannot deceive anyone into feeling unwelcome or unworthy.

THE FAMILY, THE CHURCH AND SOCIETY

As we noted in our last lesson, the kingdom of God, which is simply "the rule of God," advances in the earth in three governmental forms: (1) the family; (2) the church; and (3) the state (society). We saw these three forms of human government in the temptation of Christ in the wilderness.

However, because Christ Jesus passed the test and remained faithful to the will of the Father, He was exalted to rule over all principalities and powers, and this includes the three realms listed. Jesus is head of the family, the church and society. There are many families, churches and societies that resist this reality and seek to overthrow the rule of Christ, but each one that does so will be shattered like a potter's vessel is smashed with a rod of iron (Psalm 2:9; Revelation 2:27).

The family is the initial center of God's rule. In the beginning, God established the family as the means of taking creative dominion over the world. Adam and Eve were called to rule the world as God's agents over creation, and this agency was to be extended throughout the earth by the means of familial growth. In other words, as the human family grew in the earth, the rule of God would be extended to the four corners of the globe. The family was central to God's plan for dominion from the beginning.

Moreover, the family was the basis for the other two forms of government, the church and society. Both the church and society grew out of the basic family unit, the household. When God called Israel out and formed them into the first church in the earth, the first congregation of gathered worshippers, the first *ekklesia*, He gathered them before Him by households. The households of Israel were arranged carefully and deliberately around the Tabernacle of Moses.

Then, the firstborn son of every family was charged with the task of serving as a priest in the Tabernacle. The firstborn sons were replaced by the Levites after the sin of Israel at the Golden Calf, but the principle was still held in place by the redemption offering that each firstborn son was required to pay to the priests. In other words, from the very beginning, the ministry of the church had an organic connection with the family.

Society also arises from the family. As the family grows and extends throughout the earth, communities of families form. Households become clans and clans become tribes and tribes become nations. All of this is the natural order of societal growth, and some sort of communal and civic arrangement is inescapable.

But the family remains at the center of the development and growth. The family is the building block of all human relationships. We are born into the world as a child of parents and the sibling of brothers and sisters, and this obvious fact says more than we often see: we are defined as a person by this fundamental familial relationship. All relationships flow out of the family, for good and for bad.

This means that the rule of God must be established within the household in order for the rule of God to be established anywhere else. The rule of God within the church will only be as pervasive as the rule of God within the family. The rule of God within society will only be as pervasive as the rule of God within the family. Thus, if we wish to see the kingdom of God advance on an ecclesial and civic level, we must pray for family renewal.

SERVING AT HOME

Now, we do not have time or space here to discuss family renewal at any length. That is done elsewhere. Our particular focus here is on ministering to the family through Christian service. But we must at least make the point that family renewal is essential to the realization of the creation mandate first given to Adam and reclaimed by "the Second Man, Adam," Jesus Christ (Genesis 1; Psalm 8; Hebrews 2). And, more to the point of this lesson, Christian service is not fully Christian if it does not begin at home.

Note these biblical facts:

- Paul directly connects marriage and family relations with the relationship between Christ and the church (Ephesians 5:32).

- Paul measures a person's fitness for Christian leadership by their faithfulness at home (I Timothy 3:4).

- Paul declares that a person's responsibility to provide for their family is a matter of their faith before God (I Timothy 5:8).

- Malachi prophesies that a sign of Messiah's coming kingdom would be "turning of the hearts of the children to the fathers and the fathers to the children." (Malachi 4:6)

Each of these scriptural examples demonstrate the fact that serving one another at home is directly connected to the ministry and mission of the church. To serve is to love, and loving one another should begin with our family. It is a hypocritical parody of Christian love to serve strangers while neglecting loved ones at home.

In fact, loved ones at home must *be* loved ones, people that we love first of all. This is why God charged Israel to "honor your father and mother that your days may be long in the land which the Lord your God is giving you" (Exodus 20:12). Notice that the way children love their parents has a direct connection to the dominion they enjoy in the land. This is still true in the New Covenant age (Ephesians 6:2, 3).

Christian service is never an exotic task. This is especially true at home. In fact, Christian service at home is so ordinary that we rarely see it as Christian service. Putting food on the table, cleaning the house and changing the baby's diaper seems hardly Christian. But these things are *exactly* Christian. This sort of duty transcends mundane obligations when we catch a glimpse of the larger purpose: we are taking dominion in the land by discipling our children within our home.

Putting a Band-Aid on a scraped knee, sending a groggy-eyed husband off to work with a love-packed lunch, taking the time to talk with a teenaged son that communicates primarily with grunts and gestures—these things are the heart and soul of Christian familial discipleship, which is what the Christian home is all about. It may not seem as adventurous as feeding the starving natives of some distant land, but the starving natives in your own house will be forever changed by the way you love them through the monotonous routines of life. Christian service begins at home.

Let's look at a few texts that have to do with serving one another at home. Some of the responsibilities outlined have to do with marriage relationships, others with parenting or managing household tasks. But each of these passages shows us that we cannot divorce our faith from our family.

Ephesians 5:15–6:20

Ephesians 5 and 6 show how a married couple should love and respect one another imitating the relationship between Christ and the church. This is a long text citation, but it is worth it to read it in its entirety.

> Look carefully then how you walk, not as unwise but as wise, making the best use of the time, because the days are evil. Therefore do not be foolish, but understand what the will of the Lord is. And do not get drunk with wine, for that is debauchery, but be filled with the Spirit, addressing one another in psalms and hymns and spiritual songs, singing and making melody to the Lord with your heart, giving thanks always and for everything to God the Father in the name of our Lord Jesus Christ, submitting to one another out of reverence for Christ. Wives, submit to your own husbands, as to the Lord. For the husband is the head of the wife even as Christ is the head of the church, his body, and is himself its Savior. Now as the church submits to Christ, so also wives should submit in everything to their husbands. Husbands, love your wives, as Christ loved the church and gave himself up for her, that he might sanctify her, having cleansed her by the washing of water with the word, so that he might present the church to himself in splendor, without spot or wrinkle or any such thing, that she might be holy and without blemish. In the same way husbands should love their wives as their own bodies. He who loves his wife loves himself. For no one ever hated his own flesh, but

nourishes and cherishes it, just as Christ does the church, because we are members of his body. "Therefore a man shall leave his father and mother and hold fast to his wife, and the two shall become one flesh." This mystery is profound, and I am saying that it refers to Christ and the church. However, let each one of you love his wife as himself, and let the wife see that she respects her husband. Children, obey your parents in the Lord, for this is right. "Honor your father and mother" (this is the first commandment with a promise), "that it may go well with you and that you may live long in the land." Fathers, do not provoke your children to anger, but bring them up in the discipline and instruction of the Lord. Slaves, obey your earthly masters with fear and trembling, with a sincere heart, as you would Christ, not by the way of eye-service, as people-pleasers, but as servants of Christ, doing the will of God from the heart, rendering service with a good will as to the Lord and not to man, knowing that whatever good anyone does, this he will receive back from the Lord, whether he is a slave or free. Masters, do the same to them, and stop your threatening, knowing that he who is both their Master and yours is in heaven, and that there is no partiality with him. Finally, be strong in the Lord and in the strength of his might. Put on the whole armor of God, that you may be able to stand against the schemes of the devil. For we do not wrestle against flesh and blood, but against the rulers, against the authorities, against the cosmic powers over this present darkness, against the spiritual forces of evil in the heavenly places. Therefore take up the whole armor of God, that you may be able to withstand in the evil day, and having done all, to stand firm. Stand therefore, having fastened on the belt of truth, and having put on the breastplate of righteousness, and, as shoes for your feet, having put on the readiness given by the gospel of peace. In all circumstances take up the shield of faith, with which you can extinguish all the flaming darts of the evil one; and take the helmet of salvation, and the sword of the Spirit, which is the word of God, praying at all times in the Spirit, with all prayer and supplication. To that end keep alert with all perseverance, making supplication for all the saints, and also for me, that words may be given to me in opening my mouth boldly to proclaim the mystery of the gospel, for which I am an ambassador in chains, that I may declare it boldly, as I ought to speak. (Ephesians 5:15–6:20)

There are a couple of things to note here. First, look at how the entire household is addressed: wives, husbands, children, servants and masters. The entire household is called to live and love in a distinctively Christian way. Second, notice how the passage closes with an exhortation on spiritual warfare. This reinforces the point we considered earlier that the family is central to the advance of the kingdom of God in the earth.

I Timothy 5:1–16

In Paul's first letter to Timothy, he gives practical instruction on the family in an extended passage on the support of widows.

Do not rebuke an older man but encourage him as you would a father, younger men as brothers, older women as mothers, younger women as sisters, in all purity. Honor widows who are truly widows. But if a widow has children or grandchildren, let them first learn to show godliness to their own household and to make some return to their parents, for this is pleasing in the sight of God. She who is truly a widow, left all alone, has set her hope on God and continues in supplications and prayers night and day, but she who is self-indulgent is dead even while she lives. Command these things as well, so that they may be without reproach. But if anyone does not provide for his relatives, and especially for members of his household, he has denied the faith and is worse than an unbeliever. Let a widow be enrolled if she is not less than sixty years of age, having been the wife of one husband, and having a reputation for good works: if she has brought up children, has shown hospitality, has washed the feet of the saints, has cared for the afflicted, and has devoted herself to every good work. But refuse to enroll younger widows, for when their passions draw them away from Christ, they desire to marry and so incur condemnation for having abandoned their former faith. Besides that, they learn to be idlers, going about from house to house, and not only idlers, but also gossips and busybodies, saying what they should not. So I would have younger widows marry, bear children, manage their households, and give the adversary no occasion for slander. For some have already strayed after Satan. If any believing woman has relatives who are widows, let her care for them. Let the church not be burdened, so that it may care for those who are truly widows. (I Timothy 5:1–16)

Notice the phrase, "But if anyone does not provide for his relatives, and especially for members of his household, he has denied the faith and is worse than an unbeliever." We noted this verse above, but it is good to emphasize the practical aspect of this verse again. Providing for your family and paying your bills is a matter of faith. Those who fail to do so have "denied the faith." Providing for your family is Christian service.

Titus 2

Consider Paul's teaching on the home life of a Christian in his letter to Titus.

> But as for you, teach what accords with sound doctrine. Older men are to be sober-minded, dignified, self-controlled, sound in faith, in love, and in steadfastness. Older women likewise are to be reverent in behavior, not slanderers or slaves to much wine. They are to teach what is good, and so train the young women to love their husbands and children, to be self-controlled, pure, working at home, kind, and submissive to their own husbands, that the word of God may not be reviled. Likewise, urge the younger men to be self-controlled. Show yourself in all respects to be a model of good works, and in your teaching show integrity, dignity, and sound speech that cannot be condemned, so that an opponent may be put to shame, having nothing evil to say about us. Slaves are to be submissive to their own masters in everything; they are to be well-pleasing, not argumentative, not pilfering, but showing all good faith, so that in everything they may adorn the doctrine of God our Savior. For the grace of God has appeared, bringing

salvation for all people, training us to renounce ungodliness and worldly passions, and to live self-controlled, upright, and godly lives in the present age, waiting for our blessed hope, the appearing of the glory of our great God and Savior Jesus Christ, who gave himself for us to redeem us from all lawlessness and to purify for himself a people for his own possession who are zealous for good works. Declare these things; exhort and rebuke with all authority. Let no one disregard you. (Titus 2:1–15)

Notice again: there is a direct connection between Christian family life and the advance of the kingdom of God in the earth: the way we live brings the appearance of grace to all men (v. 11). Christian service begins at home.

CONCLUSION

We have emphasized the point repeatedly throughout this chapter, and it is a point worth emphasizing: Christian service begins at home. We have failed as a church if we are mobilized to reach every stranger in Fort Worth while passing over our own families. Peter told us in Acts 2:39 that "the promise is to you, to your children and to all who are afar off." This is still true today. The promise flows from us as individual believers to our children to the stranger. We cannot skip over our own house in order to reach the world.

In our next two chapters we shall speak about serving at church and serving in the world. But for now, we should think of ways that we can go home and serve those closest to us. What can we do to bring the love of God home to our loved ones? Think about it. Let's take Christian service home as we **WORSHIP → CONNECT → SERVE.**

CHAPTER ELEVEN

SERVING THE CHURCH

INTRODUCTION

Our goal at Cornerstone Church is to worship God, connect with fellow believers and serve those in need. We have already considered **WORSHIP** and **CONNECT**, and now we are considering how we **SERVE** as Christians. As we have considered Christian service, we have looked at how the kingdom of God comes in the world as we serve in practical Christian ministry to those in need. In other words, the kingdom of God will not be advanced in the earth by merely gathering at church to worship God and connect with one another. We must take the ministry of the saints to the streets.

As we stated from the beginning, the point of this teaching series is to help new members become oriented with their purpose and place within the church. We hope to communicate the heartbeat of this church in these lessons. Obviously, the full congregational life of a church cannot be captured on paper, and especially not in these few pages. The rich life of fully functioning Spirit-filled Christian community must be experienced to be truly known. It must come to life in more than theory; it must come alive in practice. The point in talking about Christian service is to motivate us to do more than just talk about it.

PRACTICAL SERVICE

Christian service must be practical service, and practical service puts service into practice. In other words, those who seek to serve must seek down-to-earth, practical ways of serving. There are many that love to serve in theory, but they make themselves scarce when an opportunity for practical service becomes available. Hopefully, we can avoid that trap by learning to "walk the talk." Paul emphasizes the need for transforming theoretical theology into practical service in several of his letters, the most obvious being his epistle to the church at Ephesus. He exhorted believers to "walk worthy of their vocation" and live out the implications of their faith (Ephesians 4:1).

There are others that only want to serve if their service is somewhat exotic and adventurous. Some get all fired up about taking the gospel to the Amazon jungle, dreaming wildly about standing on the backs of man-eating crocodiles while baptizing cannibal chieftains in piranha infested waters. They are quite ready to parachute into war torn nations casting out devils, healing the sick and raising the dead. But these world-shaking missionaries usually have little time for the mundane tasks of making church happen in their own community.

This sort of person often avoids little things like greetings visitors in a Sunday service, ushering guests to their seats, helping park cars for the elderly or holding an umbrella for them in the rain. Or maybe, little things like changing light bulbs, mowing grass, vacuuming the carpet, taking out the trash, serving refreshments in a church reception, or even technical stuff like running sound and lights or replacing batteries in a cordless microphone. These are the things that make church happen every Sunday. But stuff like that just seems a little too boring for the James Bond Christian. They want to change the world, not their own hometown.

Of course, this is said mainly tongue-in-cheek, but the basic idea is true. The church is filled with people that want to do great things for God; but the church is looking for people that are willing just to do the little things for God. Are you willing to do little things for God? Remember, David carried bread and cheese to his brothers before he ever won his spectacular victory over the giant. We must learn that God tests us with little tasks before he entrusts us with great ones. Do you want to minister to the world? Then, start right here at home. It is amazing the opportunities that exist all around us every day in our own local church.

FINDING YOUR PLACE

Effective Christian service within the church begins with "finding your place." There is nothing more frustrating to a Christian than experiencing a deep desire to be used of God and never finding a place to fulfill that longing. In almost every case, disgruntled Christians get that way because they cannot find personal fulfillment in contented Christian service. Involved believers are happy believers. Thus, it is in the best interest of everyone, both leaders and members, for each member of the church to find their place.

The idea of finding your place is rooted in Jesus teaching in John 14. Look at the text:

> Let not your hearts be troubled. Believe in God; believe also in me. In my Father's house are many rooms. If it were not so, would I have told you that I go to prepare a place for you? And if I go and prepare a place for you, I will come again and will take you to myself, that where I am you may be also. (John 14:1-3)

Jesus promised to go away and prepare a place for His disciples. He described this place as a "room" (or, a suite of rooms) in the Father's house. The Father's house is the heavenly temple where God dwells, which is breaking through upon the earth as the heavenly city, the New Jerusalem, that comes down from God out of heaven. This breaking-through of the heavens upon the earth will be fully consummated and completed at the Second Coming, but the process has begun already in the resurrection and ascension of Christ and the effusion of the Holy Spirit at Pentecost.

The temple of God, then, is presently breaking through upon the earth as the church; thus, the Father's house is the church. There is a place for each of us in the church, the Father's house.

So, the temple of God is the church. Yet, in reality the temple of God is even more than that. A closer consideration of the "temple theology" of Scripture shows that the temple of God exists on three levels: the temple of the individual Christian (I Corinthians 3:16; 6:19); the temple of the church (Ephesians 2:19-22); and the temple of all creation (Isaiah 66:1). We are called to find our place within the temple of God on each of these levels.

THE TEMPLE OF THE CHRISTIAN

First, we are called to find our place in the temple of our own heart. This may sound a bit odd at first, but it really makes sense when we think about it. What does it mean to find our place in the temple of our own heart? Simply to find whom we are in Christ. It is a matter of self-discovery as the Holy Spirit opens up the possibilities of personal potential, and we begin our slow, inexorable emergence from the deep existential morass of Adam's fall into the renewal of human recreation and reformation in the second Adam, Jesus Christ.

This process of self-discovery begins when Jesus takes up His residence in our heart. As Jesus teaches later in John 14, we dwell with God and He dwells with us through the indwelling presence of the Holy Spirit, the Comforter and Helper (John 14:17, 20, 23). We find our place in God as He finds His place in us. When we are filled with the Holy Spirit, God the Father and the Lord Jesus Christ come to abide within our hearts, as Jesus said (John 14:23), deep within the existential being of our soul, and we become a new "self" (Colossians 3:9, 10).

Paul draws a direct line between finding our place in the Father's house and self-discovery in II Corinthians 5. He says,

> For we know that if the tent that is our earthly home is destroyed, we have a building from God, a house not made with hands, eternal in the heavens. For in this tent we groan, longing to put on our heavenly dwelling, if indeed by putting it on we may not be found naked. For while we are still in this tent, we groan, being burdened – not that we would be unclothed, but that we would be further clothed, so that what is mortal may be swallowed

up by life. He who has prepared us for this very thing is God, who has given us the Spirit as a guarantee. (II Corinthians 5:1-5)

Our present fallen existence is like living in a tent, never quite at home, and our future glorified existence will be like moving at long last into our eternal home. And Paul is not referring merely to the outer shell of the human body. No, he is referring to the whole person that is trapped within this corruptible body, groaning and longing for the day when our present existence will explode into eternal life in a new and glorified self. In the resurrection, the whole person will be made new. Our spirit, soul and body will put on a new house, a new existence.

Some mistakenly believe that the resurrection entails the obliteration of human identity, and we shall all be absorbed into the all-encompassing life of God and surrender our individuality. This is exactly wrong. The resurrection is about being glorified, not annihilated. We shall share in the glory of God as individuals, and we shall become all that we were created to be. Our human potential will be fully realized in the resurrection. The new creation is not complete until we are recreated in the image of God and living forever as unique and diverse expressions of the glory of God.

Now, this fullness of glory awaits the resurrection, no doubt. Yet, we must insist that the future glory of believers has already broke in upon the world and upon our personal existence *here and now* through the indwelling of the Holy Spirit. The new creation has already begun in Christ's resurrection, and when the Holy Spirit comes to dwell within us, He brings a foretaste of our future glory.

In other words, we must not wait until Jesus returns to begin finding our place in the Father's house. We should not wait until the resurrection to become "at home" with our self re-born and re-formed in the image of Christ. We should not wait until the resurrection to start becoming all we were meant to be. Christ-centered, Spirit-empowered self-discovery must begin now. There is a room in the temple of the Father's house deep within our soul where the Holy Spirit has taken up residence so that we may abide with Him forever. And in the abiding, He leads us to discover all He has created us to be.

One more thing. Paul says that we groan deep within, longing to find our place. This groaning is an expression of the existential angst that we referred to above when we spoke about how frustrating it is to live unfulfilled as a Christian that never finds his place. We were created to share in the image and glory of God, and when we settle for anything less—or, when we simply cannot find our place within the kingdom of God—we experience deep frustration that makes living for God deeply unsatisfying. This is why it is so important that we spend time in the presence of God through preaching, prayer and praise, abiding with Christ and learning from Him how to become all He created us to be.

THE TEMPLE OF THE CHURCH

Second, the temple of God is the local and universal church. We are called to find our place in the church, both locally and universally, which means that we must find our place of effective, practical ministry within the church. In order to do so, we must take the time to become better acquainted with the various ministries and departments within our church.

There are numerous activities that must happen each week in order for our church to thrive as a Spirit-filled, faith community. Only by making ourselves aware of what it takes to "make church happen" each week can we get properly oriented toward serving effectively in the place that God has ordained for us.

Some think that effective Christian ministry is a matter of prolonged prayer and fasting in order to find the place that God wants us to serve, and there is no doubt that we must seek God to know how to find our place. But in reality, Christian service is not nearly as complicated as all that. We must simply examine the areas of ministry that are already functioning effectively in the church and see if we feel drawn to help in any of them.

This means that every covenant member of Cornerstone Church must understand how our local ministry is structured. Let's take a brief look at the leadership and service structure of Cornerstone Church.

Church Ministry Departments

The leadership and service structure of our church is firmly based on a New Testament framework, though, no doubt, we have worked out the details of our structure to fit the specific needs of our local church. We do not have space here for a detailed discussion of New Testament church government, but we can at least show how our departmental structure fits within the outlines of New Testament teaching.

The leadership of the New Testament church is divided into two "orders": *ministers* and *officers*. The ministers of the

154

church are the "five-fold ministry" of apostles, prophets, evangelists, pastors and teachers of the church. This order also flows out into the church in the more informal ministries of spiritual gifts, as we discussed above from Romans 12 and I Corinthians 12-14. This *ministerial order* of the church operates freely throughout the congregation as the Spirit wills.

The second order of leadership is the *official order,* and it operates more formally as the governing offices of the church. This order is also "five-fold," and it encompasses the apostle, elders, deacons, administrations and helps (I Corinthians 12; I Timothy 3). Each of these offices is active within our local church.

The office of apostle, which is simply another way of saying "missionary," is filled by the senior pastor. Then, we have a presbytery of elders that govern our congregation and take oversight of its operations and pastoral care. The presbytery of elders is served by the diaconate, which is made up of the deacons that assist the elders in governing and shepherding the church.

In addition to the deacons, the elders are served in their administrative oversight by various department leaders, which are the "administrations" of the church. Finally, there are "helps" that serve various department leaders in capacities such as Sunday School teachers, maintenance team captains, hostesses and ushers, etc.

Pause here and turn to Appendix A at the end of this book and look over the list of present church departments. This list is only a snapshot of the present ministerial structure, but it lays out a tremendous variety of ministry opportunities for each member to consider. This list is growing, and the number of those that are involved in ministry and Christian service expands continually.

There are other events and activities that occur apart from any formal organization, events that simply spring out of the life of the church. Wedding showers, baby showers, youth activities, fellowship events and outings—all of these things occur without any formal planning from an "official" standpoint within the church. But the departments listed in Appendix A are the regularly developed and maintained ministries of the church.

Opportunities for Involvement

The reason why we should be familiar with these departments is very simple. We want to give each new member numerous opportunities to "find their place" and become involved in Cornerstone Church. There is no reason to feel left out and unattached. Look through the list in Appendix A. Pray over these ministries and ask God to lead you to the area of ministry for which He has gifted you.

Everyone has a place to flourish in Christian service. This list is just the beginning of opportunities. In fact, our goal is to create a congregational environment where creativity and individual initiative is encouraged. The Holy Spirit may lead you to an area of ministry that does not appear on the list. Do not think for a moment that this means that your idea is unworthy and must be dropped. Not by any means! Pray over the idea that is flowering in your spirit, and ask God to allow the idea to blossom in vision, a spiritual vision that expands the ministry of the Body of Christ in the congregation and in the earth.

The possibilities for Christian service are endless, bounded only by the limits of our Bible-shaped, Spirit-sanctified imagination. What is your passion? Ministry in the church must be what some have called "passion-based ministry," a ministry that flows up and out of your spirit with divine unction and deep urgency.

Hopefully, the list of formal and informal ministries in this church will grow as large as the church itself, that every member may be able to express their burden and vision in a way that draws others to participate and creates endless opportunity for spiritual and emotional fulfillment in the house of God.

Ministry Advisor

One of the primary keys to "finding your place" is utilizing the service of an advisor we call a "Ministry Advisor." This advisor is one of our elders that serves both department leaders and church members in helping people find their place. The counselor is somewhat like a high school counselor that helps students determine and discover their academic goals.

The counselor is available to ministry leaders to help them find qualified and eager helpers to fulfill their ministry vision. The counselor is also available to assist members of the congregation on discovering the potential God has put within them and to help them either to be placed in a specific ministry or to develop an entirely new ministry.

Regardless of the direction God is leading you in ministry discovery and development, the Ministry Advisor is available to help you find your place. Each week, the counselor will send out an email detailing opportunities for ministry and giving testimonies of those who are finding their place and experiencing fulfillment in Christian service. Look for the emails and pray over the opportunities. There really is no telling what God will bless you to do in the kingdom of God if only you can "find your place"!

THE TEMPLE OF CREATION

The Father's house is the temple of the human heart, the temple of the local and universal church and the temple of all creation. This means that the world around us, which shall someday be made new in the resurrection, is the Father's house. As the old hymn says, "This is my Father's world."

Therefore, as Christians who live for the renewal of all things in the Second Coming, we should expect that the transformation of creation in the Second Coming has begun already in the resurrection of Jesus and in our new birth of the Spirit. This means that we should live in the world *now* as we hope to live in the coming kingdom. We should pray daily that this present world could feel *now* the life-changing effects of the coming kingdom as the will of God is done on earth as it is in heaven.

Now, we shall speak more about serving God in the world in our next lesson. But we should at least stop here long enough to say that Christians are called to minister as kings and priests in the world presently as we await the Second Coming. This understanding affects how we view the world around us. If we see the creation as belonging to our Father, if we see it as God's holy temple, then we shall work *now* to bring peace and justice to the world, though we acknowledge that the fullness of this transformation awaits the resurrection, in the new heaven and new earth wherein dwells righteousness.

Understanding that "the earth is the Lord's and the fullness thereof" brings an awareness of our redemptive role as salt and light in the world. We then begin to pray for understanding for how we should fit in this present world and where we can minister most effectively. We begin to pray that we can "find our place" in the world.

If we see this creation as belonging to the Lord and helplessly overrun by hostile, alien powers that have enslaved God's good creation, then we will see our work in the world as powerful Christian service that seeks to bring the world back to healing and wholeness through the gospel of Jesus Christ.

In the new creation, after the Second Coming, every Christian shall find his or her place. The Lord Jesus shall appoint to every believer his particular area of stewardship and responsibility. We shall rule and reign with Christ forever exploring the farthest reaches of the universe and subduing all creation to the glory of God. This was Adam's original mandate, which he perverted through disobedience. Jesus has come to redeem God's creation as the Second Adam, and we, in Christ, shall fulfill the divine destiny predestined upon man before the world began.

Jesus is preparing for us a place where we belong, a place where we fit eternally. Presently, we all feel somewhat out of place in this fallen world because we are citizens of heaven (Philippians 3:20). But in the new creation, heaven will come down to earth, and we shall find our perfect place. Thus, we should live now as the foretaste of how we shall live then.

Let us seek to find our place as Christians in the world. Let us minister daily in every day life as kings and priests that know exactly where they are called to serve.

CONCLUSION

This chapter is all about "finding your place" and serving the church in practical, powerful Christian service. God sent forth the Spirit of His Son into our hearts so that we may become the instruments of advancing His kingdom and building His church in the earth. Our goal here is to create limitless opportunities for ministry. However, all the opportunities in the world cannot replace personal, spiritual initiative. You must allow the Holy Spirit to draw you into effective Christian service. This begins as the Spirit convicts our hearts concerning the needs that surround us. Look around. Pray about the needs you see, and pray that God would birth in your spirit the form of Christian service that He wills for you.

Christian service is necessary to the growth and spiritual maturity of every believer. We cannot become the person God wants us to be if we do not find our place of ministry in the body of Christ. Our personal development depends entirely upon our willingness to

WORSHIP → CONNECT → SERVE.

CHAPTER TWELVE

SERVING THE WORLD

INTRODUCTION

In this last chapter on Christian service, we shall consider our ministry to the world. We shall consider our responsibility to minister to the world through active Christian service that is expressed in helping people in need throughout our city and throughout the world. The church is called to be "salt and light" in the world, and this means that our Lord expects His people to make a difference in the world where we live.

So often, Christians seem to think that their only responsibility to the world is to evangelize. And no doubt evangelization is the primary responsibility of the church to the world. All the blessings we can bestow upon the world in good deeds are worthless if we do not offer the hope of eternal salvation. However, we are called to do good to all people regardless of their response to the gospel. We are called to serve the world.

"NO STRINGS ATTACHED" EVANGELISM

And speaking of evangelism, for the last several years we have emphasized a particular approach to evangelism that we call "no strings attached evangelism." The idea behind this sort of evangelism is that we should minister to the needs of people everywhere regardless of their response to the gospel. We take this idea from Jesus' instructions to His disciples in Matthew 10:8: "Freely you have received, freely give." This means specifically that Jesus barred His disciples from charging "teacher's fees" for the preaching of the gospel. But it also has a larger application. We must not place reciprocal demands upon people in return for ministering to their needs.

This basic principle must undergird our approach to evangelism: we must preach the gospel and minister to the needs of people freely without demanding anything in return. And this includes intangible demands, such as church attendance or agreeing to be taught a home Bible study. Certainly we desire that everyone should respond positively to the gospel, come to our church and be converted, and if they reject the gospel and refuse to hear us we must move on to other people. But we may not make our preaching and ministry to the world contingent upon a positive response. We must freely preach and freely heal, and we must freely help those who are in need. Their response is their responsibility.

Think about how this works out in practical ministry— for example, neighborhood outreach. When we approach a home to minister in a neighborhood, we must choose our approach. The "reciprocal demands" approach knocks on the door and immediately asks the man or woman at the door to "do something" for us, as in, "come to our church," or "allow us to teach you a Bible Study," etc. This sort of evangelism opens the relationship with a demand. But the "no strings attached" approach asks for nothing—it *offers* something for free.

Thus, when we do neighborhood outreach, we freely offer prayer for those in need. When a man or woman opens the door, we tell them that we are members of a prayer team from Cornerstone Church that is ministering in their neighborhood. We ask them if they have any needs that we can pray about. We make no demands; we simply offer prayer. This means that our relationship with them is immediately established in terms of what we can do for them rather than what they can do for us. This changes everything.

This ministry approach seems to be much more effective in drawing people to our church and to Christ. In the past, evangelism has often been reduced to merely inviting people to church. Of course, we should always take every opportunity to invite people to church. But invitations to church must not be the centerpiece of our evangelistic ministry to the world. The centerpiece of our ministry to the world should be the free gift of love and life. Our ministry should be presented in terms of praying for the sick, offering hope to the bereaved, counseling the confused and encouraging the depressed.

Think of all the opportunities we have around us every day of reaching out to hurting people with the love of God. When a coworker is confiding in us about a marriage that is breaking, an invitation to church will do them little good. No, what they need is someone to minister to them right then on the spot. They do not need someone *asking* them for anything; they need someone *offering* them something, the "something" they need most, which is the love of God. If we can show people the love of God, then an invitation to church will be the easy part. People who experience the love of God in this way will often ask *you* if they can come to your church.

The bottom line is that we must rethink evangelism. We must see evangelism in terms of going out into the world to minister to the hurting. We must see evangelism in terms of Christian service. Scripture describes Jesus as one who went everywhere "doing good" (Acts 10:38), even though the ones for whom He "did good" later crucified Him. Jesus ministered to everyone around Him "no strings attached" regardless of their response to His preaching. We must do the same.

MERCY MINISTRIES

One of the most famous verses in the Bible declares, "God so loved the world that He gave His only begotten Son" (John 3:16). God's love for the world is expressed in His loving action toward the world. God loved, so God gave. We must do the same. This means that Christian love is expressed in Christian service. We love the world by ministering to the world. We love the world by putting our love into action and helping those who are in need.

There are several ways to do this. First, we should be ready at all times to minister on a personal level. We should be ready at all times to pray for the sick, to give to the poor, to offer an encouraging word to those who are down and out. Second, we should get involved with church-based activities that minister to the needy. There are numerous opportunities here in our local church to help the needy. Third, we should get involved in community efforts that reach out to the poor and distressed. This is ministry on personal, church and community levels.

Community outreach is an important part of Christian service. So often Christians have been perceived by the world as aloof and indifferent to the needs of the community. Some have seen Christians as "too heavenly minded for any earthly good." In the past many Christians have refused to get involved in community efforts for fear of being tainted by involvement with the world. However, if we can see our involvement as *outreach* to the world rather than merely *involvement* with the world, then we are better prepared to discern the role we can play and the good we can do without endangering our consecration to God through worldly entanglements.

Consider the example of Jesus Christ. He came to the world as "Word made flesh." The simple fact of the incarnation illustrates how the love of God refuses to remain aloof and untouched by the world, but rather enters into the world exactly where the world needs help the most, plunging into the suffering of the world and sharing its pain. Jesus was condemned for eating with sinners and ministering to the outcasts of society. But He refused to be intimidated by the purity police and loved the world anyhow in spite of their scorn.

Think about the marriage at Cana where Jesus turned the water into wine. That is a fairly famous story, and it highlights Jesus' willingness to get involved with the everyday needs of people. Jesus could have walked away when the need was presented to Him, but He had compassion on the couple's plight and worked a miracle that had little to do with the eternal salvation of the bride and groom. He simply loved them enough to meet their need "no strings attached." We should imitate this gracious example and help in every way we can everywhere we can.

We can help by volunteering at local hospitals. We can serve at a food bank and help distribute gifts to children at Christmas time. We can minister in jails, prisons and juvenile centers. We can visit nursing homes and convalescent centers where our prayers are profoundly appreciated. We can sponsor orphans in Third World countries. We can participate in medical missions around the world. Think of the value of investing vacation time and money in a mission to the needy rather than just taking a trip for leisure. The possibilities for ministry are endless, as vast as our sanctified imagination, as boundless as the love of God.

THE GOOD SAMARITAN

As mentioned above, many Christians have refused to get involved in community ministry because they feel that they are called to be separate from the world. They feel that their only obligation to the world is to preach the gospel and call sinners out of the world into the church. Then, they feel comfortable ministering to the needy, as long as the needy are coming to church. They feel they cannot get too involved with the world lest they forfeit their holiness unto God.

Yet there is tremendous irony here. The entire point of holiness unto God is that God's holiness might have a transformative effect upon the world. The holiness of God is *incarnational,* Word-made-flesh holiness. Jesus came from heaven to earth to show us how this is done. The entire point of being made holy is so that we may change the world around us through the impact of holiness upon the world.

The story of the Good Samaritan illustrates this point.

> And behold, a lawyer stood up to put him to the test, saying, "Teacher, what shall I do to inherit eternal life?" He said to him, "What is written in the Law? How do you read it?" And he answered, "You shall love the Lord your God with all your heart and with all your soul and with all your strength and with all your mind, and your neighbor as yourself." And he said to him, "You have answered correctly; do this, and you will live." But he, desiring to justify himself, said to Jesus, "And who is my neighbor?" Jesus replied, "A man was going down from Jerusalem to Jericho, and he fell among robbers, who stripped him and beat him and departed, leaving him half dead. Now by chance a priest was going down that road, and when he saw him he passed by on the other side. So likewise a Levite, when he came to the place and saw him, passed by on the other side. But a Samaritan, as he journeyed, came to where he was, and when he saw him, he had compassion. He went to him and bound up his wounds, pouring on oil and wine. Then he set him on his own animal and brought him to an inn and took care of him. And the next day he took out two denarii and gave them to the innkeeper, saying, 'Take care of him, and whatever more you spend, I will repay you when I come back.' Which of these three, do you think, proved to be a neighbor to the man who fell among the robbers?" He said, "The one who showed him mercy." And Jesus said to him, "You go, and do likewise." (Luke 10:25-37)

We have an obligation to do more than preserve our personal purity while refusing to help those who fall among thieves. The command to love one another includes a social setting where we are called to help the oppressed and work for justice. Christians should be leading the charge to help the homeless, feeding the hungry, campaigning for justice for those wrongly imprisoned, while working to see these people saved as a result of our efforts. We cannot see social action as an end, but it is a means to an end, the goal of resurrection. Yet, we do minister in the world "no strings attached."

Social holiness is an extension of personal holiness. It is not enough to proclaim that we are holy *personally* while refusing to extend that holy action *socially* into the world around us. Personal holiness is worked out in the world through ethics, through the way we live and treat one another. Can we truly claim to be holy while ignoring the needs of those around us? James tells us that our faith is manifest in our works (James 2). Our holiness is also manifest through our works. Jesus highlighted this when He rebuked the Pharisees for their out-of-balance concern for Sabbath regulations at the expense of those in need. Jesus made it clear that holiness (righteousness toward God) and ethics (righteousness toward men) go perfectly together. In fact, to sacrifice one is to lose the other.

We have an obligation that goes beyond mere evangelism. We must see the role we play in bringing holiness to the world through Christian service. We are announcing and anticipating the coming new creation. What does the world look like in the new creation? Is there war or peace? Hunger or plenty? Homelessness or suitable housing? Oppression or justice? Our vision of the world to come should affect how we see the world now.

Indeed, we should be working to anticipate that future *now*. Just because we understand that the fullness of new creation awaits the resurrection does *not* mean that we should sit idly by and postpone any expectation of change in the world for now. Absolutely not! The firstfruits of the new creation have already come in Christ, and we should be bringing the power of the resurrection to the world here and now every day that we live.

When we feed the hungry, house the homeless, offer job and skills training to the unemployed and language instruction to immigrants; when we work in the court systems on behalf of the falsely imprisoned (which requires mature discernment!) and reach out to the families of the incarcerated; when we go on a medical mission to Africa, or help at a Red Cross shelter during a natural disaster—the list goes on and on!—we are bringing the love of God to the world. When we minister in this way, we are ministering *as Christians in the world.*

This sort of ministry requires careful balance and strong spiritual maturity. There are two extremes we must avoid. The first extreme is what has been called "social gospel utopianism," which largely dismisses the gospel and seeks to create heaven on earth apart from repentance, baptism and Holy Spirit infilling. This is a humanistic attempt to establish the kingdom of God without God.

The second extreme is the one we most often fall into as Apostolic Christians, and it is the extreme that some have called "free church pietism." Free church pietism sees the duty of the Christian as withdrawal from the world into personal piety and purity that avoids contact with sinners as much as possible and awaits the Second Coming when all will be made new and sinners will be forever banished to hell. Both extremes are unacceptable. We must be "in the world" while refusing to be "of the world."

VOCATION

There is one final aspect of Christian service that we must briefly consider. Earlier in our study we spoke about "vocation" and how our work in the world is worship unto God. But we should think about this again and see how our vocation in the world is actually a form of Christian service in the world.

As we mentioned earlier, Christians often break their life into two disparate parts, a dichotomy of *sacred* and *secular* life. Most Christians see their service unto God as what they do at church each week, while their work is "carnal" and almost "worldly." This is flat wrong. Paul teaches us clearly that we are serving Christ when we work on the job, whatever our job may be. This is incredibly important for us to understand. We work for Christ when we work. When we get this, *it changes everything.* When we see that our vocation is unto the Lord, our work is consecrated and—if we may say it this way—filled with the Holy Ghost.

When we get this understanding it transforms our way of working in the world. We become salt and light through the work we do each day. Moreover, it changes the way we prepare our children for the workforce through sanctified career planning that boldly seeks the will of God for vocational direction. This understanding also hallows our daily activities and delivers us from the spiritual isolation that so often makes us feel alienated from God while at work in the world.

You know the feeling. You go to work in the morning, and after a full day of relentless toil, you come home feeling a million miles away from God, nearly backslidden and almost faithless. But if we can see our daily efforts as Christian service, as doing the will of God in the earth, then we will not feel like our work creates an ever-growing barrier between God and us. God is with us as we work. Indeed, He is working through us as we work, and His sanctifying Spirit hallows our labor so that it may be received as worship unto God. If we can see this, then our entire attitude toward our work is transformed and the alienation from God is overcome. Vocation is Christian service.

CONCLUSION

The story of Mary and Martha and their conflict over "serving Jesus" versus "sitting at the feet of Jesus" helps bring Christian service into proper perspective. This story follows immediately after the story of the Good Samaritan in Luke 10.

> Now as they went on their way, Jesus entered a village. And a woman named Martha welcomed him into her house. And she had a sister called Mary, who sat at the Lord's feet and listened to his teaching. But Martha was distracted with much serving. And she went up to him and said, "Lord, do you not care that my sister has left me to serve alone? Tell her then to help me." But the Lord answered her, "Martha, Martha, you are anxious and troubled about many things, but one thing is necessary.

Mary has chosen the good portion, which will not be taken away from her." (Luke 10:38-42)

There are two things to note here. First, Jesus made it clear that sitting at His feet to worship and to be taught His Word is "the good portion." This establishes the priority of worship and the fact that service that does not flow from worship is invalid service. This helps us avoid the pitfall of the "social gospel." Second, Jesus did not rebuke Martha for her service, but rather for her anxiety about her service and her failure to properly evaluate Mary's act of worship. No doubt Martha was troubled by Mary's presence among the men because of the cultural norms of that day which banned women from male-dominated religious discussions. Jesus corrected this notion and accepted Mary as a full participant in His lessons.

However, the salient point for our discussion here is that Jesus was not rebuking Martha's service. He was simply placing it in its proper context. We must do the same. We must hold worship in its proper place at the head of Christian experience. Christian service must flow out of Christian devotion and Christian fellowship. In order to **SERVE** properly, we must first **WORSHIP,** then **CONNECT,** then **SERVE.** Or, as we have depicted it throughout this series, we must **WORSHIP → CONNECT → SERVE.**

MEMBERSHIP COVENANT

The covenant mission of Cornerstone Church is three-fold. First, we covenant together to **WORSHIP** the one true God in such a way that all nations will come to worship Him as God revealed in Christ through the Holy Spirit. Second, we covenant together to **CONNECT** with one another in such a way that we truly edify the body of Christ and meet the needs of those Christ has saved. Third, we covenant together to **SERVE** our family, our church and the world in such a way that the love of God in Christ through the Holy Spirit is truly actualized in the real world.

APPENDIX A

The following is a list of current church ministry departments (administrations and helps) that operate in our church. This list is somewhat fluid, and it expands and contracts depending on the ministry needs of the church. Study this list to "find your place" by the direction of the Holy Spirit. Remember, the Ministry Advisor is available to help you work though finding where you fit in local church ministry.

- Benevolence
  - Care for the needy within the church
  - Care for the needy outside the church
  - Food pantry
  - Clothing closet
  - Charity events
- Bookstore
  - On location bookstore
  - Online sermons
- Bus ministry
  - Sunday School routes
  - Spanish service routes
  - Regular service routes
- Business ministry
  - Job's Roundtable
  - Leaders In Business
- Children's ministry
  - Sunday School
  - Bible Quizzing
  - Choir
  - Drama

- o Child Development
- Couples Ministry
  - o Under 40 Couples' Ministry
- Drama
  - o Youth drama
  - o Adult drama
- Finance administration
  - o Board of Directors
  - o Treasurer
  - o Finance administrator
  - o Finance secretary
  - o Weekly deposits
- Fundraisers Team
- Hospitality
  - o Guest ministers
  - o Receptions and fellowships
  - o Coffee shop, Sunday morning refreshments
  - o Decorating
  - o Ministry to widows
  - o Meals for the sick, new mothers, bereaved
- Hostesses
  - o Greeters
  - o Guest relations
- Maintenance
  - o Building maintenance
    - ▪ Weekly upkeep of buildings
    - ▪ Scheduled workdays
  - o Grounds maintenance
    - ▪ Weekly mowing
    - ▪ Monthly landscape maintenance
  - o Cleaning teams
    - ▪ Weekly cleaning schedule
- Media ministry
  - o Sound
  - o Lighting
  - o Projection

- o   Audio recording
- o   Video recording
- o   Online content
- Ministers In Training
  - o   MIT Class
  - o   Online training
- Music Ministry
  - o   Worship
    - Song list
    - Musicians
    - Singers
  - o   Chorale and Choir
  - o   Talent development
  - o   Outreach events
- Outreach
  - o   Mobile church
  - o   Jail/Prison ministry
  - o   Canvassing
  - o   Mailers
  - o   Home Bible Studies
  - o   Visitor follow-up
- Patrol
  - o   Security
  - o   Crossing guard
  - o   Cadet patrols
    - Valet parking for elderly
    - Umbrella service
- Public worship service
  - o   Service schedule
  - o   Service leaders
    - Readers
    - Exhortations
    - Speakers
- Publications
  - o   Website
  - o   Outreach fliers

- o Sunday bulletin
- o Daily devotions
- o Weekly announcements
- o Sermon and lesson handouts
- o Books
- o Writers Guild
- Secretarial
  - o Pastoral secretary
  - o Administrative secretary
  - o Finance secretary
- Shepherd's Guild
  - o Attendance
  - o Follow-up
  - o Pastoral care
  - o Ministries placement
    - Ministry Advisor
- Singles' Ministry
- Spanish Ministry
  - o Spanish service
  - o Outreach
  - o Pastoral care
- Special Events
  - o Festivals
  - o Camping trips
  - o Retreats
  - o Outings
- Ushers
  - o Guest relations
  - o Security
  - o Offerings
- Youth
  - o Youth class
  - o Youth events
  - o Drama
  - o Youth Ministries Team
  - o Parents' Council